THE
ANGLER'S BOOK
OF
FLY TYING
AND
FISHING

THE
ANGLER'S BOOK
OF
FLY TYING
AND
FISHING

Howard Goldberg

CHARLES SCRIBNER'S SONS, NEW YORK

Library of Congress Cataloging in Publication Data
Goldberg, Howard.
   The angler's book on fly-tying and fishing.
   1. Fly tying.   2. Fly fishing.   I. Title.
SH451.G64   799.1   73-1338
ISBN 0-684-13377-6

1 3 5 7 9 11 13 15 17 19 C/MD 20 18 16 14 12 10 8 6 4 2

Printed in the United States of America

DEDICATED

To
My Wife
Barbara Joan Goldberg
Without whose help this volume could not
have been written and who looks
kindly upon
my sporting endeavors.

To
My Father
Nathan Goldberg
Who during my fourth year
introduced me to all that accompanies the
Sport of Angling, and who was
an angler's angler, up until the last.

To
My Late Uncle
Jack Goldberg
Who will always remain in my memory
as an inveterate angler and
Sportsman of the highest order.

ACKNOWLEDGMENTS

No author can write a book totally on his own. There are always people who have influenced the writer's thinking and philosophy. In addition, there are the many in the wings who directly or indirectly play their part in helping with the production. It is to all of these people that I am deeply indebted.

Keith Fulsher and Charles Krom. This book could have never been written without the help and knowledge of these two angling sportsmen. They have been a constant source of help and knowledge and have given unselfishly of their time. They have also provided many of the tying techniques illustrated here. This book is really as much theirs as mine.

Harry and Elsie Darbee, who took the time to help me with my fly-tying problems, served as a source of fine materials, and helped with tying processes.

Charles De Feo, who gave of himself, showed me many tying tricks of the trade, and provided me with samples.

Alan B. Dietz, who took the time on that park bench a few years past in New York City to help me with my first angling literary piece, and who was an early source of encouragement.

Mark Sosin and Milton Rosko, who have been angling and literary companions, and who have been free with the exchange of information.

Richard Dietz and Richard Dietz, Jr., who have been sporting companions afield.

Robert and Glad Zwirz and the Angler's Cove was a magnificent gathering place, source of information and cracker-barrel-style discussions. It is a pity that it is no longer.

To William C. Steinkraus, whose thoughts, ideas, and suggestions have proved invaluable.

To the many other tiers whom I have had the privilege of sitting next to, and watching work. I owe them much for what they have taught and shown me.

To the students that I have taught, and what they have taught me in the process.

To my photographic laboratory, Motal Custom Darkrooms, who made all of the prints for this book.

And to Grace von Stein, who did all of the typing and proofreading.

CONTENTS

INTRODUCTION

The making of one's own fishing flies has to be one of the most interesting and challenging aspects of angling. This is the skill which helps one become a complete angler. Fly tying gives a depth to the sport that is hard to obtain in any other way. For the angler who makes and fishes his own flies the satisfactions are great indeed.

When one takes up fly tying, he can't help but become something of an entomologist in the process. Insects upon which trout feed must be studied to be imitated. It isn't long before the newcomer knows aquatic insects by both their scientific names and the common names used by anglers. Insect life cycles are also included in the learning process.

A similar fund of knowledge is built up concerning birds, and the animals which are utilized by the fly tier. In short, fly tying opens new dimensions of indoor and outdoor activities—all related to angling.

Those who are dedicated to the conservation of wildlife have been critical of the fly tier because he uses feathers and furs from the world's most beautiful and rare birds and animals. Most of these materials, however, are by-products of food processing, the fur trade, or other such industries. I have met but few anglers who were not conservationists in the truest sense of the word and genuinely interested in the preservation of all wildlife. Anglers are first to give of their time and talents in this field, especially when it comes to improving water quality and better fish management. They practice the "no-kill" and "trophy fish" policies promoted by sound conservation groups. And are happy to return home after a day of fishing with nothing in their creels but the memories of a day afield. The remembrance of a beautiful trout slowly swimming away, unharmed, after being tricked by an artificial fly of one's own creation played in pure water, and released to provide more sport in the future is reward enough.

Fly tying is not difficult to learn and can be self-taught easily with the aid of a proper book on the subject. Unfortunately, even though fly fishing is one of our most written-about sports, there is little which has been done to help the beginning fly tier get off to a good start. Because of this, I was extremely pleased to learn that Howard Goldberg was to write this book. As an expert fly tier and fly fisherman he knows well the sport; as a photographer he is unexcelled. These things, together with his skill as an out-doors writer, make him a natural for doing this overdue book.

A sharp photograph can easily show a technique that pages of words can-not describe. After reading this book, I think you will agree with me that the emphasis Howard has put on the photography goes much further than just illustrating the text. He has clearly pictured the little tricks that make the difference between success and complete frustration.

Furthermore, each style of fly is covered as a unit so that you can work on a particular grouping, be it wet, dry, or streamer, without wading through a myriad of material.

We are part of a burgeoning world. Within most of us who love and enjoy the fast-moving streams of the diminishing outdoors lies a strong desire to associate with the wilderness of the past—the wilderness of men who lived by their knowledge of the forest and stream, and the animals and fish that lived in them. Fly tying provides an opportunity to turn back the hands of time and associate momentarily with that era—and once again catch and play a trout from memories past.

January 1972

Keith Fulsher
Eastchester, New York

▲▲▲▲▲▲ CHAPTER 1 ▲▲▲▲▲▲

FLY-TYING
TOOLS

Whether you are a newcomer to the art of fly tying or a seasoned professional, fly tying offers you, the angler-tier, the means of extending your regular season to include the whole year through.

Very few tools are actually needed to make well-constructed trout and salmon flies. In fact, the fewer carefully chosen tools you use, the better. Over the years, my own outfit has evolved to include the following basics: vise, hone, hackle pliers, two pair of scissors, bobbin, tweezers, dubbing vise, hone, hackle pliers, two pairs of scissors, bobbin, tweezers, dubbing needle or bodkin, hemostats, razor blades, and thimble. Purchase the best-quality tools you can afford. The best are not expensive and with care will last several lifetimes.

With the foregoing complement, I can make virtually every kind of lure—ranging from large salmon and streamer flies to the smallest of midgets. Even the best tools play a very minor role in making well-tied flies. Good-looking, properly constructed lures are mostly the result of combining high-quality materials, a sense of design, and the balance and skillful dexterity of the dresser. The last factor is, by far, the most important.

Gadgets are *not* important. The real key to gaining experience is to keep your tools simple, so that you can concentrate on improving your skills. As the fledgling tier gains experience, new items can then be added to his tool box when he finds them necessary.

Besides a vise to hold your hook securely and a dubbing needle for performing countless tasks, a small hone for pointing up hooks should also be a must. Each hook should be inspected prior to tying to ensure that barb and point are sharp.

VISE

The most important tool is the vise. It wasn't too many years ago that fly tiers used only their fingers to hold the hook during the construction process. But as the art progressed, tools were designed which speeded up the various operations and allowed the newcomer, after little effort, to make flies that are as good as or even better than those tied by hand.

There are several good vises on the market. Like most items, some are made and function better than others. I have used the Thompson Model "A" lever type with the clamp mount for years. In my opinion it is one of the best.

The Thompson Model "A" is fully adjustable for height and has a base "C" type clamp for fastening to the tying bench. Its tapered vise jaws are made from hardened steel and are fully adjustable to accept hooks ranging from the very large to the very small. The lever, which works on a camming action, holds the hook securely. To release the hook, simply flip the lever. By controlling the tension on the lever when the hook is in the vise-jaws, the fly can be rotated so that the opposite side or bottom can be worked on.

DUBBING NEEDLE

I made my own dubbing needle from a large darning needle stuck into a cork wine bottle. It has served me admirably. If you want to be real fancy, you can buy a ready-made one. Tackle and fly-tying shops do offer them for sale. I use mine to apply lacquer to the silk head, remove dried lacquer from the hook-eye, and pick out hackle or dubbing that should get covered during the tying process. It is a most universally useful tool indeed.

HACKLE PLIERS

Hackle pliers are another very important tool. They should be able to handle the finest hair or hackle without breaking it. They should also fit the hand so that the tier can work quickly and smoothly. Before his death Herb Howard made and sold hackle pliers which are the best that I have ever used. These pliers are still being made by Danville Chinelle Co. and are sold through retailers such as Orvis.

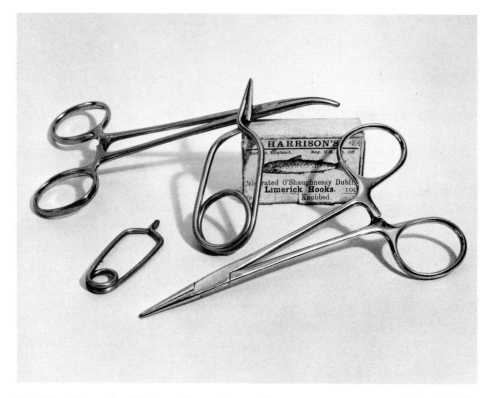

Hackle pliers should have jaws that will grasp stems and quills securely, yet without breaking. Curved- and straight-jawed hemostats have proved ideal for grasping larger materials and acting as an emergency vise.

HEMOSTATS

Hemostats are a tool which fall into the luxury category. My wife, being a nurse, first recommended them to me as possibly being of some use. She was right; now I would never be without a pair. They fit a variety of purposes, from holding materials out of the way during the tying process to pinch hitting as an emergency fly-tying vise out in the field. If you are going to get a pair, I recommend the smallest size as fitting the widest range of uses. They are available in both straight- and curved-jawed varieties, either of which may be chosen.

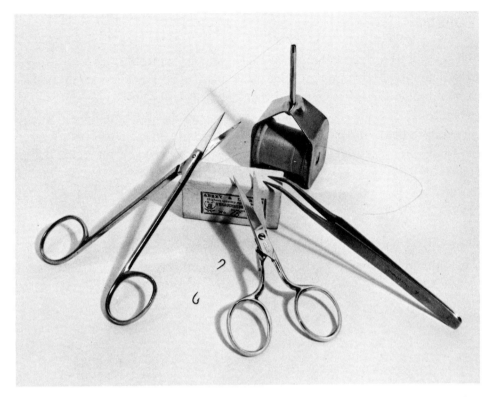

When tying, bobbins are a definite help in controlling the tying silk. For all your cutting needs, use fine- and broad-bladed pairs of scissors.

SCISSORS

The fly tier should have two pairs of scissors. I prefer both pairs to have straight blades. For cutting coarse materials, floss, tinsel, and for trimming heavy hair bodies, I use a small pair of mustache or embroidery scissors. The second pair should have ultra-fine points and be the best quality cuticle or eye surgeon's scissors obtainable. I do all of my fine cutting work with this pair. Surgeon's scissors can be gotten from a local surgical supply house, but be prepared to spend a few extra dollars. Though they are expensive, in the long run they're worth it. Being made from the best materials they last considerably longer.

BOBBIN

Choosing the right bobbin is a great help in controlling the silk thread. A bad one is an abomination. There are many good fly tiers who do not use a bobbin; however, I have found that I can tie faster and more consistently when using one. Check the following when purchasing a bobbin: it should fit comfortably in the palm, have some method of controlling thread tension, and have no rough edges on the guide to cut. I use the all-metal bobbin made by S & M Fly Tying Materials, of Bristol, Conn.

TWEEZERS

A pair of tweezers, capable of picking up small trout hooks, is needed. One in which the jaws will have a firm grip and stay closed with little pressure is ideal.

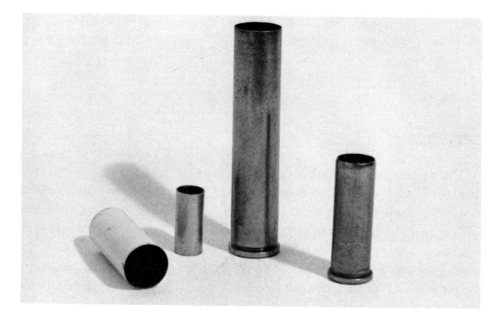

Lipstick tops, spent cartridge cases, and ferrules can be made into thimbles.

RAZOR BLADES

Single-edged razor blades are a must for the serious fly tier. The super-sharp edge can be used to cut materials neatly and closely. That same edge can also be used to strip poorly tied flies which do not measure up to your standards from hook shanks.

THIMBLE

A thimble from the top of a small lipstick container, spent cartridge cases with glue-filled flash holes, or an old rod ferrule is an idea tool for evening up the ends of hackle, fur, or bucktail. The thimble was first shown to me by the great artist-fly tier Charles De Feo. I would never be without it.

CHAPTER 2

FLY-TYING MATERIALS

Fly-tying materials are the very foundation of tying. If the tier is ever to reach the professional level of tying competence he must come to know the different materials and how they are used. For any fly, regardless of how skillful the maker, can only be as good as the materials from which it is made. Poor or mediocre materials can only result in lures of the same quality. Best-quality materials look well, can be fished to best advantage, and will be durable. Such materials also help the tier by working easier and laying on faster for him.

Learning to judge materials is an art unto itself, which can best be learned by experience. If you are a newcomer, my best advice is to begin learning about materials by deciding which fly type you first want to make. The dry, wet, nymph, and streamer all take about the same degree of skill. Then, make up a materials list of several chosen fly patterns. Tie these patterns and gradually expand those which call for new materials. In this way, it won't be long before you will be able to tell at a glance or touch if items meet your standards and fit your needs.

If you order your materials by mail, only work with dealers who have a return privilege. If, for instance, when you order by mail, a dealer is temporarily out of a particular material, he should so notify you or send a substitute on approval. If the substitute doesn't meet your needs, simply return it as it was received. With reputable dealers, you can be assured of getting the quality paid for.

A reputable dealer will help the fly tier; his future business depends upon it. I have personally ordered materials from such dealers as Harry and Elsie Darbee of Livingston Manor, N.Y., Eric Leiser at the Fireside Angler in Melville, N.Y., and Reed Tackle in Caldwell, N.J., and know them to be reputable.

This book is directed toward the angler-tier who wishes to imitate the fleeting impression of real insects. Of most consideration is a fly's color, shape, and silhouette. Just as, if not more, important is how that fly works when it comes in contact with the water. Materials tend to change color when wet or when treated with a wetting or floating agent. If you are trying to achieve a particular color shade, match it as it is intended to be fished.

TYING THREAD

The purpose of the tying thread is to fasten all parts of the fly to the hook. Today's tier uses thread made from pure silk or nylon, which ranges in size from "D" (used for heavy salt-water flies and rod wrapping) to 8/0 fine (used for super-delicate work when tying small midges). Using the correct thread size is important. If the diameter is too fine, the silk will break when the slightest pressure is applied; if too coarse, it will create unnecessary bulk and not look proportionate to the size. For most of your regular trout and salmon fly-tying work you will be using 6/0 or 4/0 thread. Thread also comes in a variety of colors and is pre-waxed.

WAX

Wax is applied to tying thread to increase its working strength and adhesion. In the case of pre-waxed thread, extra wax can be applied when fur dubbing and other materials are to be attached to the thread. This is accomplished by first warming a small piece of wax by kneading with the hands until soft and then rubbing the soft wax onto the thread.

LACQUER

Lacquer is necessary for finishing off the fly's head after the thread has been whip-finished. I use airplane dope for this. It penetrates and dries in the thread rapidly, and comes in a complete range of colors. It is also readily available in small quantities from most hobby shops; this reduces evaporation over long periods when the lacquer is not in use.

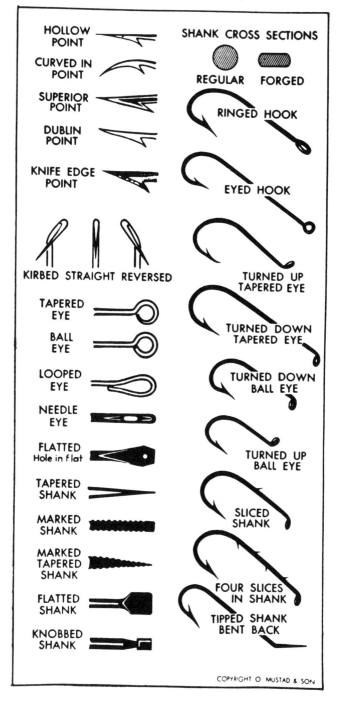

COPYRIGHT O. MUSTAD & SON

HOOKS

The species of fish, its habitat and habits, the methods of angling employed, and the type of lure used dictate which hook model should be used. A hook suited to one set of circumstances may be completely wrong for another. Each fly type calls for its own set of hook specifications.

I like the Norwegian Mustad trout hooks more than American, English, or other manufacturers'. These are bronze finished. For my salmon flies, I prefer the English-made hook with japanned finish. This finish resists the rusting qualities of brackish water well.

If dry flies are being tied, I use Mustad's number 94840 standard fine-wire hook with tapered turned-down eye. For late-season, low-water trout fishing, I use Mustad's number 94833, which is the same as the 94840 model except that it is made with 3X-fine wire. For wet flies I use Mustad's number 7948A, made from standard wire which has a turned-down tapered eye. For fishing the nymph, simulating its emergence, and meeting other regular and low-water conditions, I use Mustad's number 9672. When conditions dictate that I go deep in heavy water, I use weighted flies tied on the same hook. For my standard streamers and bucktails, I prefer using Mustad's number 9672, which has a turned-down tapered eye and a 3X-long shank, or number 79580, which has a 1X-long shank. For my reverse head Thunder Creek minnow imitations, I use ring-eyed Mustad's number 9674, with a 4X-long shank. For my salmon flies, I use the standard and low-water japanned, black, loop-eyed English hooks. For dry salmon flies, I use the Wilson fine-wire hook.

TINSEL

Tinsel is used to rib or form whole fly bodies. It can be purchased in many styles and sizes; these include flat, embossed, oval, wire, thread, and twist. The most commonly used colors are gold, silver, and copper. Make certain to obtain a type which doesn't tarnish.

A synthetic called Mylar has been on the market for a few years now and I have had a chance to test it. Mylar doesn't tarnish, is very light in weight, holds up well, and has proved to be a new body and wing innovation. It is available from hobby, knitting, or sewing supply shops in sheet, flat ribbon, or piping form. It is quite easy to work with. The braided piping has an inner core of cotton threads which can be easily removed. The hollow braided Mylar tube is then slipped over the shank of the hook. The braided Mylar makes a beautiful, realistic minnow's body.

FLOSS

Floss is available in real silk, nylon, and rayon. It is usually single or double stranded. It is ideal for making fly bodies. It can also be used as an underbody in shaping wet flies, nymphs, and streamers. Used as an underbody, I apply several coats of lacquer and wrap my body material over it while it is still tacky. The added weight of the floss underbody has proved ideal for weighting subsurface flies.

CHENILLE

Heavy and medium chenille is used for wet-fly bodies. It comes in a wide variety of solid colors. The sparse type is ideal for making egg sacs since it is of light weight and has a minimum absorption. Silk chenille is the best; it gives lures a thick fuzzy shape.

FUR AND WOOL DUBBING

Dubbed bodies made from animal fur or processed wool yarn is one of the oldest, most effective, and attractive means of making fly bodies. Almost every variety of animal fur is available to the tier. Even special shades can be blended by combining different fur or wool colors.

For dry-fly bodies, the best furs to use are those which do not absorb water readily. For the most part these water-resistant furs come from animals having some contact with the water. They include beaver, muskrat, fox, seal, otter, raccoon, badger, and mink.

Doing some late-season varmint shooting a few years back, I was able to get a full-coated red fox. By skinning and curing, without tanning the skin, I have been able to retain all of the natural animal oils. Dry-fly bodies made from this fur have proved almost unsinkable.

The colors on a full red fox skin range from gray, to red, to buff, and to pink. When I wish to blend in some brown, I use beaver. If a deep grayish tint is wanted, I use muskrat. The best furs for dubbing are found close to the skin. Unless a shaggy body is wanted, it is best to remove the guard hairs after removing the fur from the skin.

Furs used in tying wet flies should absorb water as quickly as possible. Local small-game wild animals such as rabbit, squirrel, and even sheep have fur which is ideal for making dubbed wet-fly bodies.

Swatches of the different animal skins are available from your local fly-tying material store or mail order house. It would not hurt to also make the acquaintance of the furrier in your neighborhood. You would be surprised what can be picked up from the clipping-room floor.

SPUN FUR AND WOOL

Spun yarn, made from pre-twisted fur and wool fibers, saves the tier much time. It is easy to work with and precludes the need of spinning a fur-dubbed length for each fly body. Pre-twisted fur and wool body materials are different from yarns found in knitting shops. They are finer, looser in twist, and generally fuzzier.

Spun body materials (made from synthetic and natural fibers) are available in a variety of colors from most fly-tying material houses. If you want to make your own, to match a particular fly you will be tying a lot of, E. H. "Polly" Rosborough in his book *Tying and Fishing the Fuzzy Nymphs* shows how blended furs are prepared and made into wool noodles. The only drawback I've found when using spun materials for fly bodies is that it necessitates using another material to imitate body taper. Spun body materials are relatively uniform in diameter.

Fur strips are another method of making fur fly body materials. It combines the best of the dubbed and spun material principles and is easily manufactured. Fur strips can also be tapered by regulating the amount of fur used—and easily stored until needed by winding onto cards.

To make these strips, take a 12- to 14-inch length of tying thread and wax it well. Lay the thread across your knees. Clip or tear small sections of fur from the skin and place over half the length of the waxed thread. By regulating the amount of fur spread, you can make a natural taper. Be a bit stingy with the fur; a little fur goes a long way. Double the thread over the fur so that it is sandwiched between the two halves of the tying thread. Roll the whole sandwich in one direction only across your knees or between your palms. In the beginning, the tendency is to use too much fur. Experience will tell you the correct amount of fur to use. Store your fur-dubbed strips in a cool dry place.

PEACOCK FEATHERS

Peacock feathers are a commonly called-for fly-body material. They are either shimmering metallic green or bronze in color and become very lifelike when wet. Peacock eyes are the large multicolored tips of the peacock tail feather. It is named for the eye-like spot in the center of the round tip. Stripped of their fuzz, the eye quills make excellent dry-fly bodies. Left on the quill, the fuzz imitates nymph gills when wet. The herl found on the stem of the peacock tail feather also makes an excellent body material. Tie in three or four herls together, and then twist to form a single strand before winding around the hook's shank. Herl from peacock sword (body) feathers is also used in making fly tails and wings.

CONDOR QUILL

Wing quills from the condor have wide, two-color fibers which make excellent fly bodies. The colors range from white to dark liver. Like the peacock eye quill, the fibers must be stripped of their fuzz.

PRIMARY WING QUILLS

Primary wing quills from wildfowl, turkey, domestic goose, domestic duck, swan, pheasant, grouse, woodcock, as well as from other species of birds, are ideal for making fly wings. In tying these wings, cut identical segments from a matched part of left- and right-wing quills. Place the backs of the convex surfaces together so that the points are even. Grasp between thumb and forefinger, determine the length wing you want and the point at which your thread will grip the wing butts. Hold the wing over the shank of the hook at the point you wish them to be tied in. Pull or skillfully work the thread between your thumb and forefinger with the thread looped over the point in which you wish the wings tied in. Now, the trick is to squeeze the wings and at the same time pull straight down; loop again before releasing to ensure that the wings are on firmly. If the fibers of each wing are lying one on top of the next and are not folded over, you have the wings on correctly. If the wings are tilted off center, release the thread and do them again. The same tying procedure is used when sections of primary wing quills make up fly tails. However, instead of two quill sections, only one is used.

MOOSE MANE

The moose's mane is made of coarse durable hair ranging in color from white to brownish black. The hair is hollow and tough, and makes neat segmented fly bodies when dark and light strands are wound together around the shank of a hook. This material can also be used to simulate nymph and large wet-fly legs.

PORCUPINE QUILLS

Porcupine quills make smooth buoyant dry-fly bodies. Each quill is hollow; they range in color from white to brown, and must be flattened by pulling between the thumb nail and forefinger before being tied into the hook shank.

PLUMAGE AND TAIL FEATHERS

Almost every male bird's plumage and tail feathers can be used to make flies. Dry flies seldom require fancy plumage from birds foreign to the United States. What is required of feathers used in dry flies is that they absorb as little water as possible. Duck and other waterfowl plumage have proved ideal for this purpose.

Many of the wet-fly patterns, however, call for different kinds of brilliantly colored fancy feathers. When choosing feathers for wet-fly patterns, they should be selected for their ability to absorb and to give a lifelike appearance under water—as well as for their color, quality, texture, and size.

Feathers have always been the bane of the fly tier's existence. Often, certain feathers called for in specific patterns are hard to get, and when you *can* get them, they are not of the quality needed. When I run across such situations, I try to change to a similar material. For example, many popular trout patterns call for male wood duck lemon-colored flank feather wings. Wood ducks are hard to come by; even hunting them is a very uncertain situation. I very often substitute bronze mallard body plumage. It matches so well that I seriously doubt if the trout can tell the difference.

A very good source of feathers are friends that hunt, if you don't. I find that the body plumage of local wild game birds such as pheasant, grouse, woodcock, and quail make excellent wet-fly nymph and streamer hackle. Fibers from tail feathers can also be used to imitate insect legs and tails.

HACKLE

The fly tier and angler both consider hackle one of the most important, controversial, and sought-after materials used in the making of trout and salmon flies. This is especially evident when one considers hackle quality with regard to its ability to float dry flies. Not all fowl produce hackle feathers suitable for use in the best dry flies.

Good stiff, water-resistant, dry-fly hackle with little or no soft web can only be obtained from mature roosters or game cocks. The birds grow hackle only about their neck and saddle. Hen hackle is useless because it is too soft and absorbs water, which sinks the fly. Climate also plays an important role. It seems that, for dry flies, hackle is at its best during the cold winter months.

The best hackle to use in the making of dry flies are those with long, narrow, glossy fibers which are almost even in length. The hackle's underside should be just a bit lighter in shade, with a slight sheen to the fibers. Regardless of color, good, first-quality dry-fly hackle is always in demand. There are just not enough good necks to go around.

Genetics are responsible for making some natural hackle colors exceedingly hard to find in the better dry-fly quality necks. The blue dun color, for example, is obtained from Andalusian cocks bred from pure white and black parents—not blue dun ones. Mating blue dun to blue dun will not yield blue dun offspring; the bluish gray color is recessive, and recessive genes don't breed true. This also means that the quality of the feathers will not be as high as in dominant-colored birds. Usually you will find color *or* stiff hackles—finding both is luck. Even after you have found a natural blue dun neck, was it worth the time and money spent? I have my reservations.

To the conservative old guard, I'm about to put my neck on the proverbial chopping block by saying I don't believe color in most instances is as important as other contributing factors—*providing* the color is a natural one and a similar shade can be found on live insects.

All of my dry flies are tied as sparse as possible. Flies fished in high, fast, rough water need more turns of hackle than ones used on slow-moving, low-water streams. Use just enough hackle to float the fly. The philosophy "if a little is okay, more is better" doesn't hold here. Over-hackling causes the fibers to absorb and hold water like a paint brush. In most instances, I consider the amount of hackle used more important than its color.

The color range found in feathers used in hackling artificial flies is wide and varied. Today, the trend in fly tying is to blend different colored hackles rather than to try to match a specific colored feather to the wanted shade. With the following shades, the tier can tie almost every pattern: black, dark mahogany, brown-medium, ginger-light, grizzly-light and dark, medium blue dun, white, and the different mixed "bastard" colored hackle.

Most of my dry flies are tied with these mixed multicolored hackles. As a rule, they are less expensive. They are also stiffer and make better dry flies. Because the colors are mixed, two different "bastard" colored hackles can be blended to make a rich impressionistic hackle.

Just as important is selecting hackle for wet flies, and streamers and legs for nymphs. These flies do not need to have the stiff springy hackle necessary for dry flies. In choosing wet-fly hackle, look for soft, water-absorbing feathers. Twitched through the water, these feathers pulsate and give the appearance of life.

HAIR

The hair from various animals is suitable for dry, wet, and streamer flies. Hollow hair from animals of the deer family is ideal for wings and tails of dry flies, provided it can be found fine enough. The Wulff series of dry flies was the first to make use of hair as a floating material in insect imitation. Making use of hair enabled the fly to support a heavier body, created a good sturdy-looking wing, and built a fly that could be used for fish after fish with no more attention than a quick glance while false casting. The hair also allowed the fly to be fished in heavier, faster water without it sinking.

I have also used the fiber found on a woodchuck's tail as the tail of dry flies. This material works well, is easy to find, inexpensive to purchase, and comes in a variety of colors.

Wet-fly wings and tails can be made from any animal with solid hair, including deer and impala, calf, and the guard hairs from the different species of fox, bear, and goat. Squirrel hair is a durable material which stands up under hard use.

DYEING MATERIALS

Very often, it is impossible to find the desired shade of a particular color. If you want that color, you must get it by dyeing. I am not a great advocate of dyed materials, especially of dyed hackle. Most hackle, when dyed, tends to become brittle, dull, and lifeless, with the fibers losing their trans-luscence.

The best dyes I have found are those used to dye cloth. Before dyeing materials, read and follow the instructions which come with the dye. Mix the dye in a container which won't pick up the color. Place the dye in a small amount of boiling water, making sure that all dye particles are mixed thoroughly into solution.

Material about to be dyed must be washed in strong hot soap to remove grease and dirt. Pre-soaked materials which are still wet absorb dye faster than dry materials. Usually materials need only stay in the dye a very few minutes. The trick of dyeing materials is to watch the quill, taking care not to let it get too dark. Materials should be taken out just short of the shade desired. Most materials, when dry, darken. If they are lighter than desired when dry, you can always put them back for a few additional seconds. Make sure to set the color so that it is permanent, and then press out the remaining moisture between paper towels and allow to dry.

STORING MATERIALS

With the price and scarcity of quality materials these days, careful storage is a must. Necks should be stored with a stiff piece of cardboard, so that the skin lays flat. Place both the cardboard and neck in a clear plastic envelope, large enough so that it can be folded double. The fold acts as a seal. Being in clear plastic, each neck can easily be identified. Keep all of your necks together in a single container with a liberal amount of moth crystals.

I separate all of my different furs, tinsels, floss, wools, threads, and other materials individually, in shoe boxes. The boxes stack nicely, and, being labeled on the end, materials can easily be found when needed. About the only material in fly tying that you can use a great deal of without getting into difficulties is moth preventive flakes, crystals, and balls. Use it liberally.

⋀⋀⋀⋀⋀⋀ CHAPTER 3 ⋀⋀⋀⋀⋀

THE DRY FLY

An angler hasn't lived until he has experienced what it is like to be in the middle of a hatch occurring at full force. I'm not talking about one or two insects one often sees floating or flying by as they struggle to become airborne, but rather a blizzard of wings, so thick he can't see beyond the end of his rod. Such happenings always bring out the big fish, fish that cast all shyness aside, rolling, charging, and jumping after insects who are in almost total control of the current. Such is the stuff of which angling dreams are made.

Since its inception, the dry fly was intended to imitate insects floating on or in the surface film of the stream. Dry-fly fishing was invented by the English angler Frederic M. Halford on the river Test around 1880, as a way of attempting to take trout when other methods failed. It has since had many improvements, enjoyed many fads, and today is still one of the most popular methods of trout and salmon fishing.

In 1890 Theodore Gordon introduced Halford's new angling method—the dry fly—to American waters. Gordon, a sickly man, lived and fished the Catskill Mountain country of New York State. He became interested in the new angling approach through the British angling publication *The Fishing Gazette* while convalescing.

Gordon, like his English counterpart, felt frustrated when his sunken fly failed to take fish when hatching mayflies were coming off the water. Emulating Halford's methods, Gordon's first attempts at making floating flies and fishing them on an upstream drift were a failure. He was still using standard wet-fly patterns, tied on heavy wire hooks, and made of materials as absorbent as a sponge. Halford initially evolved a set of thirty-three dry-fly patterns. These were reputed to have been painstakingly copied from live insects and supposedly so exact in detail that even the sex was accounted for. It is interesting to note that all of the original thirty-three patterns had wings. Included were three pairs of male and female mayflies, eleven male and twelve female spinners, three sedges, and an ant. In his book *Dry-Fly Fishing in Theory and Practice,* published in 1889, he expanded his set to include other lesser insects.

The two anglers corresponded regularly. Gordon requested and Halford willingly sent a complete sample dry-fly series. *This was the beginning in the United States.* These first samples revealed Halford's use of materials, methods, and techniques. Copying the English patterns, Gordon again met with failure. Correspondence suggests that Halford's imitations found on chalk streams didn't have similar corresponding ones on American streams. Gordon quickly realized that if he were to enjoy the same success, he would have to tie patterns which imitated American insects.

Without sounding like an angling heretic, in my opinion Gordon didn't achieve the degree of success anticipated because his dry-fly fishing techniques, methods, and equipment lacked the necessary refinements. The fly patterns had little or nothing to do with his catching or not catching trout. I in no way wish to belittle what Gordon accomplished. It must be remembered that any inventor with nothing but intuition to guide him very often goes through a long trial-and-error period before finding success.

Of the many patterns Theodore Gordon originated, the one which bears his name is still the most popular—the Quill Gordon. To this day still, he is considered the Father of American Dry-Fly Fishing.

The bulk of the average trout's diet is made up of mayflies. At times, stoneflies and caddisflies also play an important role. Given streams, or even a particular locale, may often have still other insects—like the green inchworm hatch of the East and the big salmon fly of the West.

One year, on a favorite meadow stretch of a quiet mountain stream that I fish regularly, the red-legged March fly first mentioned in Charles M.

Wetzel's book *Trout Flies* was a real hot number—particularly when a breeze came up. The wind blew these terrestrial insects which happened to be in multitude that season off the bank in great numbers. When that occurred, big trout went wild and dashed about in the open with reckless abandon.

To the angler, the most difficult part of angling is deciding what fly to use. Here, money will not help in the decision-making. To be successful, the angler must understand that at streamside circumstances are never static. Conditions are constantly changing. To compound the angler's dilemma, a little way up or downstream a completely different set of circumstances governs. Learn to use your eyes, and the stream will become like an open book.

Dry flies to be effective must be made from the fish's point of view. Much of that effectiveness is comprised of color, shape, silhouette, and floating qualities. Live insects are not opaque, they are translucent. It is this as well as color and movement of materials which suggests life.

Three is no doubt in my mind whatever that natural furs produce the most translucent-appearing bodies. The reason for this is that very small bubbles of air are entrapped in the hair fibers and project life into the fly as it moves on or through the water. Quill-bodied flies are almost as translucent as fur. Hackle, too, should reflect light. I prefer to use natural undyed materials and hackle, because they reflect light better. Shape and silhouette are also important. You can use the finest materials, and if your lure doesn't simulate what you're representing it to be, the trout caught will be sparse.

To begin your fly-tying practice I suggest that you decide upon one dry-fly pattern. The first goal is then to learn to tie it well before going on to others. Almost all flies have the same components, that is, body, tail, wings, and hackle; only different materials are used. For simplicity's sake, let's begin with the Cahill pattern. Besides meeting all of our requirements, it is made from relatively inexpensive materials.

Even with your first fly-tying efforts, set your standards high. If a fly doesn't meet your criteria, be ruthless and strip the materials from the hook. To do so will make you a better fly tier faster. Using the step-by-step pictures showing correct procedures you should have little difficulty, even with your first efforts.

When you can make a dozen flies perfectly, you can consider yourself proficient. One of your first urges will be to experiment with some wild creations. Don't! Instead, tie patterns which are popular in your area. If possible, work from well-tied samples of other local anglers. Local and published patterns very often differ, their only similarity being in the name. I'll wager the taking fly of the two is the local one.

Place a size 12X fine-wire Mustad model number 94840 hook in your tying vise so that the barb is fully exposed.

The wings are the first part of the fly to be attached to the shank of the hook. Their placement is important. It governs the proportions of the whole fly. If, for instance, the wings are attached too close to the eye, there will not be adequate room when it comes to wind on the hackle. The correct point at which to tie in the wings can be easily determined by running two imaginary vertical lines, which are perpendicular to the shank of the hook. The line at the left should cross the shank just behind the eye. The line on the right should cross the shank before the bend of the hook begins, and also the barb. These two lines determine the main trunk of the fly's body (1). The wings are placed one third of the body's length behind the eye.

Build a foundation for the wings by winding on waxed tying thread around the shank where the wings are to be attached (2). This is necessary so that the windings will not twist loose after the wings are attached.

The Cahill dry fly calls for a divided wing made from a portion of a lemon-colored male wood duck's flank feather. Two good substitutes are mallard breast feathers, dyed to match the lemon color, or bronze saddle feathers found on the male mallard's saddle (3).

Take a portion of the feather chosen and roll it into a cylinder between thumb and forefinger. The length or height of the wing will be equal to the just-determined body length of the fly. With the feather between thumb and forefinger, place it in position on the shank (4). Still holding the wing material, bring the tying thread between the thumb and wing. Now loop the thread over the feather wing and bring it between feather and forefinger so that it forms an inverted U. Pull your working thread straight down, then bring it around the shank and repeat a second time before releasing the wing. The wing is now secure, and lying on top of the shank (5). Lift the wing, so that it is perpendicular to the shank, and wind tying thread around so that it forms a wedge between the shank and wing. This forces it to remain perpendicular. Not many turns are needed to force it to stand upright.

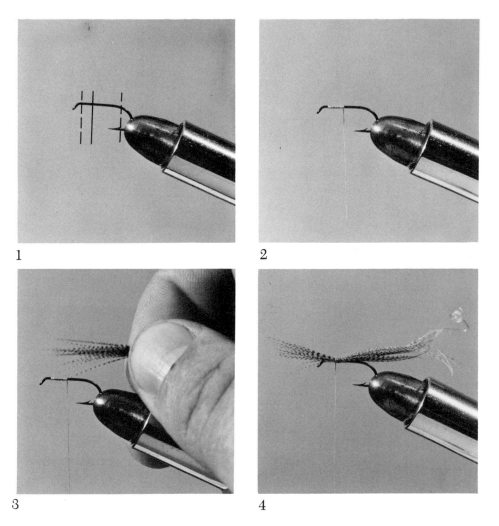

1

2

3

4

Divide the wings by splitting in two equal parts with your tying thread, figure-eighting it between the wings so they are anchored into proper position. Clip excess material (6).

Wind the thread back to the point where the tail is to be attached (7). Take a few long stiff—and I mean stiff—medium ginger saddle or neck hackles and tie them by using the same procedure as with the wing (8). The tail fibers should be at least as long as the body. Take care to use many fibers. For the average dry fly tied on a size 12 hook about seven fibers are

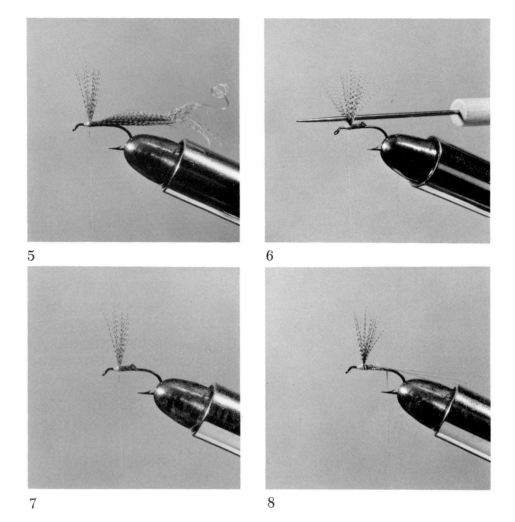

5

6

7

8

sufficient. Larger-size flies should have a few more fibers. Care should be taken, however, not to use any more materials than necessary. Heavy tails absorb water like a paint brush rather than float the fly on the water's surface film.

The Cahill dry fly calls for a yellowish gray body. To get the proper shade, I blend a small amount of the reddish fox fur found on the neck and shoulders with the gray fur found on the chest. Take care to be sure that all guard hairs are removed before blending. Stack the different furs together and

9   10

hold them between thumb and forefinger. With the other hand, gently pull
the fur; repeat several times, until the fur is blended together. Prepare the
thread with an extra coat of wax to ensure that the dubbing (fur fibers)
will stay attached to the thread while the body is being formed (9). I like to
taper my fly bodies by using less fur at the ends of my dubbing noodle.
Spin the fur between thumb and forefinger in one direction (10). A back and
forth movement will not spin the fibers onto the thread. Now, wind on
dubbing, taking care not to overlap coils of fur (11). Be sure to end the body
so that enough room is left bethind the wing to provide adequate room for
the hackle. If your dubbing noodle is longer than needed, end the body by
separating with thumb nail and forefinger.

Select two stiff, medium-ginger-colored hackle feathers having the same
length fibers as the gape of your number 12 dry-fly hook. Select feathers
having little or no web. Strip them of their fuzz, and make a scissor cut on
each side of the stem. These cuts should be 90 degrees to the natural lay of
the fibers. Just below these cuts make a third cut perpendicular to the stem
which you then sever. What results is a wedge shape formed by the cut
fibers (12). When tied in, the hackle is keyed and locked into place so that it
can't pull loose. Nothing is more frustrating than to get one hackle wound
on, then to start on the second one and have the feather pull loose.

Take both prepared hackle feathers and place them shiny side to shiny side, and align the butts so that they are even. Put them into position as illustrated and take three turns with the tying thread to anchor them into place (13). Grasp the tip of the feather closest to the eye with the hackle pliers and make three complete turns with the hackle behind the wing. Make another turn, crossing the hackle underneath so that when completed it is in front of the wing. Make three more turns and tie off the hackle (14). Repeat the process with the second hackle (15).

11

12

13

14

For the average dry fly size 10 through 14, that is to be used under normal water conditions of midseason, takes a total of seven turns of hackle. For larger sizes or flies to be used under heavy fast-water conditions, increase the number of turns as needed. For smaller sizes or flies to be used when the water is low and the fish extra wary, decrease the number of turns. Adding more material than needed does not help a fly float.

Form the head by taking a few additional turns with the tying thread. Care should be taken to use fewer turns than you feel the completed head will need. Room must be allowed for the whip finish (16).

Completing the fly with the whip finishing knot is easy. There are tools on the market supposedly to help the tier do this. However, I have found that they hinder rather than help. To tie the whip finish by hand, take the thread between the thumb and the third finger and wedge the standing end (free end) between the working part of the thread and thread-wrapped head. Release the standing end and wrap only the working thread about the shank five turns. After making the turns, contain the thread with dubbing noodle so that it can't unwind from the shank. Grasp the standing end and pull straight back. Doing so will take up all slack and form a knotless, neat-looking head.

Apply a drop of clear airplane dope to the head with your dubbing noodle. Let dry and repeat the procedure (17).

15   16

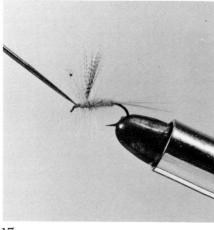

17

Another popular wing used on dry and wet flies is made from the primary wing feathers of waterfowl. If purchased from fly-tying material houses, they are usually sold in matched pairs of whole wings. A matched pair consists of the same primary wing quill taken from each wing. Both are usually the same length and width and have the same compound curvatures.

In tying these wings, cut identical segments from right and left quills. Place the backs of the convex curve (top side) of each segment together so that the points are even (1). Pinch between thumb and forefinger. Determine the length of wing wanted and the point at which the thread will grip the wing butts (2). Tie them on using the same methods as with the rolled wing. On the dry fly the points usually point upward (3) (4).

If the wings are tilted to the side, do them over. They should ride on top of the hook and should not be folded. Hold the wings perpendicular to the shank and start winding the tying thread in front (forming a wedge) to raise them to a vertical position. When vertical, wind a few figure-eight loops to keep the wings separated.

Still another wing style is made using hackle tips, which are fast replacing wings made from primaries. They are strong, and if tied correctly will out-last the full life of the fly's use. In preparing the tips, hold them so that their points are even (5). Establish wing length and carefully strip the hackle fibers from the stem. As with the other types of dry-fly wings, place the feathers bright side to bright side, and use the same procedure for tying them in (6).

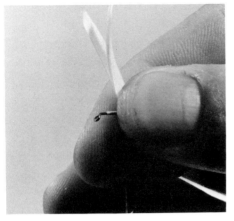

1

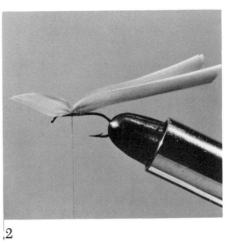

2

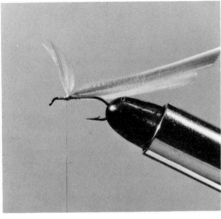

3

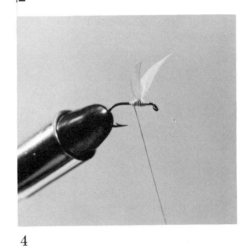

4

5

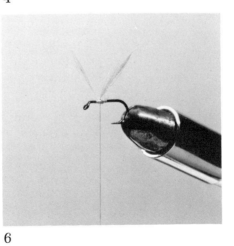

6

For late season, low-water fishing I like to tie small dry flies using the same feathers for the hackle and wing. The advantage of using the same feathers for both is a less bulky fly. Having less turns of material and thread, the fly of course is lighter. Take note that because the hackle is wound on first, prior to forming the wings from the tips, all of the hackle is going to be behind the wings. You may also have to adjust the number of turns on the second hackle, one or two turns less, to get the wings to come out even. Another reason for using this tying method is that perhaps you are imitating an insect having dun-colored hackle and wings. Natural blue dun is a bit too expensive to be making into just wings. This method allows you to use the same feather for both.

For real rough-water fishing in the spring where insects are hatching but the water is strong and fast, and regular dry flies don't perform up to their usual standard, I switch to hair wing patterns. Some animal hair—deer hair, for example—is hollow. Because it is hollow, when it is tied in, the air inside is trapped—helping to make an almost unsinkable fly. Other hair, such as impala or calf tail, also makes excellent wings and tails. For the newcomer, working with hair can be a problem, especially when it comes to lining up all of the ends of the hair so that they are equal. Charles De Feo showed me a neat and easy way of always making sure that the ends are even. Take a top from a small lipstick container and put the amount of hair you're using into it. Swirl the hair around to separate the fibers and then tap the bottom of the container gently on your work table top. If care is used in taking the hair out, all of the ends will be even. Take the Hairwing Royal Coachman as an example. Tying a hair wing is almost the same as tying the rolled feather style wing. Because the butt ends of the hair are heavier than feather fiber butts, when it comes to clipping them, cut them on an angle so that the hair butts taper. For heavy wings it is often advisable to put a drop of airplane dope on the butts prior to cutting them off. The dope anchors the fibers.

The hopper fly is another which has well proven its worth to me. I primarily fish this fly from the end of the spring through the summer—or whenever these insects are prevalent. The grasshopper imitation which I prefer is the one having a solid quill body. They are easy to make and almost indestructible.

Begin by taking a turkey or peacock tail feather and cutting off the white part of the stem where it was attached to the bird. If you use a knife to perform the task, make sure to cut at an angle. If a perpendicular cut is made, you are apt to split the stem.

Begin with the tying-in of the tail. Next, do the body and then prepare two hackle feathers so that they become self-locking. Tie in both hackles and advance the thread to the tying-off position.

Wind one of the hackles with the number of turns specified and tie off. Instead of clipping the hackle point, which is the regular procedure, build a wedge of thread under the hackle point to lift it perpendicular to the shank.

Now, wind on the second hackle fiber, planning it so that when complete it will be as long as the first wing part. Because you are tying over the additional material of the first hackle, the second will not have the same number of turns as the first, that is, if both hackles are of the same length prior to winding on. Experience will tell how much additional length is needed on the second hackle.

HAIR WING ROYAL COACHMAN

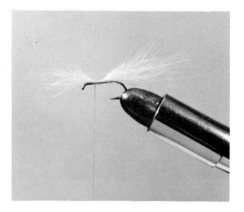

Tie the hair fibers on top of the shank and place a drop of cement at the point of the windings. Clip the fiber butts.

Lift the wing and with the tying thread build a suitable wedge to anchor the hair wing into place. If the wing can move about the shank, remove and start again.

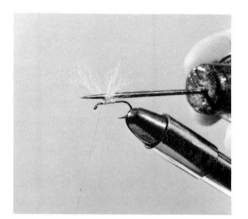

With the point of your dubbing needle, split the wing into two equal parts and prepare to figure eight the wings.

After making your initial figure eight, place a drop of cement at the junction of the two wings. Complete your wing separation and wind thread back to the tail position.

For the tail of the Hair Wing Royal Coachman tie in a few golden pheasant crest fibers. Clip the excess butt material.

Next, to form the tri-segmented body of the Royal Coachman, take several strands of herl from the peacock tail feather. Break the weak tip sections of the herl and tie in. Twist the strands together to form a single working strand. Wind tying thread several times around the twisted herl to keep it from unwrapping. This adds strength to the herl and keeps fish teeth from slicing through the herl body. With the prepared herl strand, wrap one-third of the body and tie off.

Clip the excess herl, tie in some red
floss, and wrap the middle one-
third of the body with the floss.

Tie off the red floss. Care should
be taken to keep the body as flat
as possible. There is a tendency for
the floss to bunch if the tier is not
careful.

Keep as much tension as possible
on the floss and use as much tension as the tying thread will bear
when tying off.

Wrap the remaining third of the
body with herl, repeating as before.
End the body with enough room
for the hackle turns fore and aft
of the wings.

When completed, the herl floss- and herl-banded body give the impression of a real insect's segmented body.

Next, select two fiery brown neck hackles from a Rhode Island red rooster having the right length barbuals and tie in. Be sure to place the hackles shiney side to shiney side.

Wind hackles on individually. Place the first hackle as close to the wing as possible. Wind the second hackle through the first, taking the last wraps in front of the first hackle.

Complete the fly by clipping the unwanted hackle tip, forming the head, using the whip finish, and applying several coats of head cement.

Since most stems are a milky translucent white, they can be colored to any desired shade by painting or dyeing. I prefer the dyeing process because the stem retains its translucent character.

Insert a small cork into the end of the stem to make the body watertight. Use small round corks found in most tackle supply catalogues. Get ones that are slightly oversize and fit them individually. Use glue to secure the corks to the quills. Prepare a size 1 or 16 hook with a 3X-long shank by wrapping with pre-waxed thread. Anchor the quill on the hook shank with tying thread. For legs, cut two smaller quills and tie to the sides of the body quill. These smaller quills are important. They add stability to the floating fly by acting as pontoons. If your bugs are to be painted rather than dyed, paint them now and add two hairs of moose mane for antennae. Your imitation grasshopper is now complete.

Another type of insect imitation which I like to fish during low-water conditions is the Japanese beetle or jassid. The jassid type of artificial trout lure utlizes the flat wing style where the feathers lie over and the full length of the back. When tied sparsely, they float *in* rather than *on* the surface film of the water. Although originally made with jungle cock eye (nail) feathers, which are now protected, other feathers can be used in their place. Generally, these flies are made on small (18-22) size hooks. Select the proper small-size hackle to match. Strip off the fuzz and trim the stem's butt. Tie in at the rear of the hook shank and wind the thread forward toward the eye. Take care to wrap the tying thread evenly over the shank so that no metal shows. The thread forms the body. Tie off the hackle and trim the fibers extending from the top and bottom of the body. If done properly, it will extend only from the sides of the body. It is these hackle fibers which float the fly in the surface film of the water. Select one large or two smaller jungle cock or other feather types and lay them over the body so that the convex side of the feather is up. Tie the feathers in at the eye, form the head, clip the tying thread, and add finish to the head. Your fly is now complete.

Another unusual body material, which is not used as often as it should be, is the hackle stem. It comes in a variety of colors, floats well, and will stand up well under heavy usage. Soft wet-fly hackle stems seem to tie in better than the stiffer dry-fly hackle stems.

Prepare hackle stems by first stripping off all fibers. Then, immerse the stems in water overnight. They will float but at the same time absorb water. The trick is to get them soft, so that they can be wrapped about the hook's shank without splitting.

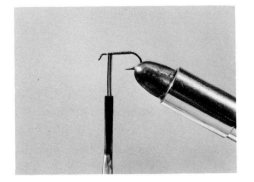

Still another very useful quill can be taken from the eye of a peacock tail feather. The fuzz is stripped off with an eraser, revealing a flat, light-colored quill with a dark edge. This is the quill used in making the Quill Gordon. To protect it from being cut by sharp teeth, a fine coat of lacquer can be applied or gold wire counter-wrapped.

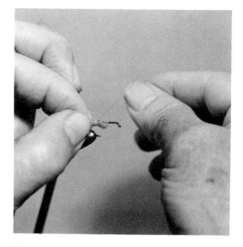

Hollow animal hair can also be utilized in making floating dry-fly bodies. Here, deer hair is spun about a dry-fly hook.

The secret of tying deer hair-bodied flies is to tie in small bunches of hair, spinning it about the shank, and when the body has been completed, trimming it to shape.

The completed body ready for trimming. Note that adequate room has been left on the shank for wings and hackles.

Of all types of lures used in fly tying and fishing, the dry fly is the most popular. It affords the angler a means of taking trout when they are on the rise and when water conditions are such that subsurface lures tend to hang up on the bottom. Learn to tie dry flies well and you won't have any difficulty tying any of the other lure types. I consider the dry fly when tied properly the most difficult of all fly types to make.

There are three insect orders upon which trout do the majority of their feeding: caddisflies, mayflies, and stoneflies. Of the three, the mayfly is the primary food. Trout also feed on other insect orders such as ants, Western grasshoppers, Eastern inchworms, and beetles which through some local situation happen to fall in the water with any degree of regularity.

In the East, for example, inchworms become trout food by eating the leaves of trees which overhang streams. This usually happens toward the end of May or even into early June. At such times, with the help of wind and/or rain, the trout quickly learn to lie in wait for falling insects. At such times, it takes a well-controlled lure to entice them to take anything but an inchworm imitation. The inchworm is a difficult insect to imitate. About the best I have found is deer hair tied about the hook shank (similar to the Rat-Faced McDougall but clipped extra short). The hair should be dyed to match

THE TWO-FEATHERED FLY

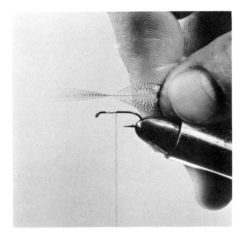

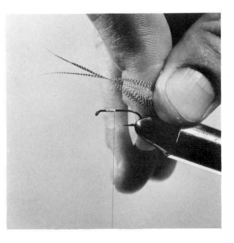

The two-feathered fly with the tail, body, and wing made from the same unbroken feather is begun by reversing the direction of all but six or eight wood duck or wildfowl body feather fibers.

These six to eight fibers are split into two groups. A small spot of lacquer on the tip of a dubbing needle is touched to each section. This forms the tails.

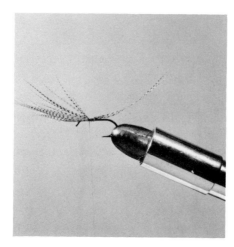

Next, with the fibers reversed, the feather is tied to the shank of a dry-fly hook, forming the lure's body.

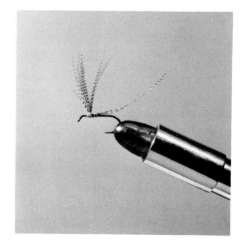

The wing fibers are now wedged perpendicular to the hook's shank. They are then divided and figure eighted to anchor them into position.

Two light blue dun hackle fibers are keyed into position and wound on. The fly is then finished in the conventional manner.

The two-feathered fly offers the angler a fly which is very light in weight. It is perfect for late season or low-water fishing.

the greenish brown of your local species, as the color varies from locality to locality.

Caddisflies, mayflies, and stoneflies spend almost all of their life cycle under water. For this reason, trout do the great majority of their feeding below the surface. Minnows are another popular food form which is also found below the surface.

The winged fly on the surface of the water suggests the adult stages of life. Generally there are four stages in the life cycle of these insects: egg, larva, pupa, and adult. It is only when the urge to reproduce occurs that the insect rises to the surface, dries its wings, and leaves the water. In this stage, little food is eaten and mostly air is breathed. It usually alights on foliage, makes its last molt, and again flies off—this time in search of a mate. After the acts of fertilizing by the male and laying by the female, with the eggs being deposited on or beneath the water's surface, both adults die.

▲▲▲▲▲ CHAPTER 4 ▲▲▲▲▲

THE WET FLY

Old things are often the best. It is that way with the wet fly. The angler who is after larger fish should investigate wet flies. Large trout, for the most part, take insects below the surface of the water. They leave the surface stuff for the smaller fellows. The basis for all wet-fly techniques is the imitation of nymphs and minnows or the simulation of what looks like food to the trout.

The dividing line of wet-fly patterns is clear: there are those patterns which imitate natural food while others serve as attractors, imitating no living thing. To me, the wet fly proves to be most effective when fished as an emerging insect about to leave its watery home. As such, I stay close to those patterns which imitate. The attractor patterns may work in an area which doesn't receive a great deal of pressure, but it's hard for me to imagine a trout preferring these to natural-looking insects.

Almost everything in wet-fly fishing technique is based on the water to be fished. Pattern choice, size and style of fly, rigging the leader, and methods of presentation all differ with the type of water to be fished. I find, for the most part, that big flies mean big fish. You may get fewer but they will be bigger. Big flies are usually tied on heavy hooks. As such, they go deeper faster, even in spring water which usually runs fast and deep. In light-water streams where the runs and pools are fairly shallow, not more than three feet deep, and the rocks small, the flies can also be smaller.

Before presenting your wet flies, the lie of the fish should be known. This includes understanding the feeding habits of fish in a particular section of water. Generally, when trout are seeking food in the form of underwater insect life, they will assume a position near the head of the pool or run. They will lie right in the rush of fast water, near a large rock for protection, as the water breaks into the hole. The important point to remember is that they will seldom venture far from the water bringing food into their home pool or fast-water run. A trick my dad showed me of long ago has proved effective. The biggest trout in a pool will occupy the choicest lie. Take that fish and another almost the same size will replace the one caught in a short time if conditions are right.

The length of the rod is important in wet-fly fishing. Generally, when fishing big water, a longer rod allows better control and action of the flies. When fishing streams and rivers under shallow-water conditions, a shorter rod is of benefit.

There are two important methods of fishing the wet fly. The first is the cross-stream cast and retrieve. I work the water in the following manner. I take a position slightly above and across stream from the area I want to fish. The flies are cast and dropped above this area, and they are not allowed to sink. As the flies touch the water, the rod is lifted, to keep as much of the line as possible from dragging, and the flies are fluttered across the fish with a rapid shaking or palsied motion, and retrieved rapidly. At the same time, a fast switching motion is given to the flies with the rod tip. Such a technique makes the top dropper fly of the cast literally skim the surface of the water. This technique is extremely productive when the trout are rising freely to the floating, fluttering, natural insects or emerging nymphs just about to hatch. It is the most effective heavy-water technique that I know.

When this technique proves to be ineffective, I take the same position as before, that is, slightly above and across from the area I want to fish. I let the flies sink through the action of the current. When the flies have progressed to the desired depth, I begin a slow twitch of the flies. As the current begins to straighten the flies I again give a couple of small tugs to the line, then release it to the current. When the line and flies are directly below me in the current, and still no fish has taken my offering, I begin a twitch-and-hold technique until all of the line has been retrieved.

In wet-fly fishing, the size of the fly is governed by the type of water to be fished, its color, and its flow. Also to be considered is the size of the natural insects and the shyness of the fish which inhabit the stream you're working. I lean toward large flies and use a fly of a size which I am certain will be readily seen by the fish, considering the color of water and the nature of the stream.

The wet fly is tied to represent one of the following insect conditions: a rising pupa about to emerge, a drowned adult fly, a female submerged in the act of depositing her eggs, or small crustaceans or insect life.

When constructed properly, the wet fly embodies the following: water-absorbing materials, sparseness, a hook heavy enough to sink the fly, silhouette, color, and flash. Water-absorbing materials help the fly to sink and are usually soft enough to give the movement necessary to represent life. Sparseness allows the materials to pulsate and work naturally. Standard and heavy wire hooks help the fly to sink fast. To take fish with the wet fly, you have to get the fly to the fish. Lure silhouette is important. In the half-light of stream shadows, I am convinced it is the deciding factor of a trout taking or not. Colors must closely represent the naturals. Care should be taken when choosing materials as certain materials change color and character when they become wet. Be sure that the colors are matched. Flash is comprised of reflections from shiny materials such as tinsel and reflections caused by air bubbles clinging to portions of the fly itself. For life-imitating lures, ones which take trout consistently, flash is a prerequisite.

The trick of floating the wet fly is suspending it at the right depth. It should not bump the bottom. Doing so will only foul the fly. The fly should move with the current, suspended and portraying lifelike action through manipulation and control of both rod and line. To do it successfully takes skill, not the kind needed to cast on a nice flat green lawn. Here there is little in the way of room, brush and tree branches get in the way, and there are slippery rocks and strong uneven currents to contend with.

The wet-fly fisherman fishes by instinct. To be successful, he must be able to visualize in his mind's eye where his flies are and anticipate difficulties before they occur. The imitative trout lure must portray the image of fleeting food about to be swept downstream. The better that the angler can accomplish this feat, the more trout he will take regardless of what his lure looks like. Attaching a fly having the proper silhouette will improve "luck" further. In my opinion, color plays little if any part in enticing the strike in the murky shadows of dark water. Once an angler becomes skillful with the wet fly and nymph, he'll take fish when other methods fail.

One of my favorite wet flies is the Gold-Ribbed Hare's Ear. If I were limited to one single wet fly (I hope it never comes to pass) for all of my wet fly angling, unequivocally I'd choose this fly. It looks buggy when wet. I have had more luck with the Hare's Ear than any other. But then again, I've fished it more than any other. We tend to fish better with lures we have confidence in. I am no exception. I feel that confidence in a particular fly is as, if not more, important than the pattern itself.

Confidence is transmitted to the fish in several ways. First, in the selection of specific materials by the tier-angler. Then the manner in which those materials are utilized in the construction of flies. This predetermines how the fly will work when submerged. And finally, the manner in which the angler controls the fly in the water.

Since the dry fly has been mastered, the wet should offer no new tying difficulties. In construction, the wet fly is infinitely more simple. Let's take my favorite wet-fly pattern, the Gold-Ribbed Hare's Ear and follow me as I tie it.

To begin, take a standard fine wire Mustad wet fly hook and wrap tying thread about the shank. Wind toward the rear until the thread is in position for the tail to be tied in. Select a few brown hackle barbules for the tail. Use the thimble even and to align all barbule points. The length of the tail is equal to the distance between the shank and barb of the hook. Tie them in so that they spread slightly. Next, tie in some fine oval gold tinsel for the rib. When this is accomplished, extend the tinsel out of the way so that dubbing can be applied to the tying thread. Clip and mix dark- and light-colored hairs from the mask and ears. On most flies when blending dubbing, I remove all the guard hairs after clipping the fur from the skin, but with the Hair's Ear, I omit this step. Blend and dub the fibers on the waxed thread. Care should be taken to taper the dubbing so that when wound on the shank, a tapered body will be formed. Be sure to leave adequate room for the wing and head.

With the body now wrapped on the shank, I spiral the oval gold tinsel to form the rib. This is done against the lay of the body. In so doing, the tinsel locks in the fur and keeps it from being chewed by the fish. With the tinsel now in place, pick out the heavy and longer guard hairs to form the lure's legs with a dubbing needle.

Next, take a pair of wings clipped from matching left and right mallard duck wing quills, and face them so that both wings curve inward and lie against one another. The wings should curve downward. Pinch the wing between thumb and forefinger, set into proper hook shank position, and tie in. This is accomplished by first bringing the thread between thumb and wing, leaving slack in the thread, and then looping it over to the other side and slipping it between wing and forefinger. The objective here is to pull straight down with the tying thread. This forces the material between tying thread and hook shank in a pinching motion. If the thread is applied in a wrapping motion, the material being tied in tends to spin or rotate about the shank in the direction the thread is being rotated. Thread slack and material looseness can't be avoided.

There are two means of applying wet-fly hackle. I use both of them, depending upon the effect I want to achieve. The first is similar to winding on dry-fly hackle. After winding in and tying off, the hackle is stroked downward to form a beard under the shank. Thread is then wound over the top of the hackle windings until the hackle stays at the desired angle.

The second method of applying wet-fly hackle is to finish the fly to the point where the wings are tied in. All that remains is to tie in the hackle, form the head, and finish with lacquer. With the wings tied in, flip the fly on its back. It's much easier to apply the hackle beard upside down. Select suitable wet-fly hackle and stroke the fibers perpendicular to the hackle stem. Select the amount of fibers necessary and clip as close to the stem as possible. Position under the wing, and tie in. Use the same pinching method as with the wing. If tied in correctly, the hackle beard should flair naturally, and achieve the correct angle.

In the first hackle process, the hackle seems to be a bit fuller. Hackle fiber length must be predetermined before winding on, while hackling with the second method allows the tier to adjust the hackle length to meet his own requirements. I always seem to have more larger hackle than smaller. This proves an ideal way to use up my excess larger material.

Form the head with tying thread and use the whip finish to tie off. Apply several coats of head lacquer, taking care to let each dry before applying the next.

There are several other types of wings the tier should become familiar with. Each has its purpose for imitating natural insects. The wing style mentioned on the foregoing Hare's Ear is called a closed down wing. The open down wing is the exact reverse. It is made by taking the matched mallard wings, clipped from the bird's primary wing feathers, and facing them so that the wings curve outward away from each other. The tying in process is the same.

Hackle tips can also be tied down wing. And, as with the wildfowl primaries, they can be tied either open (shiny side to shiny side) or closed. Hackle tips can also be tied flat over the body beetle style.

Rolled wet-fly wings are also popular. They can be made from most species of upland and waterfowl body plumage. Body plumage from the various species of our game birds gives the tier a wide range of colors and shade variations with which to create new patterns to meet local conditions.

Rolled wings are made by spreading a body feather so that the fibers extend perpendicular to its stem. Pinch a desired amount and cut from the stem. Roll this pinched amount of fibers between thumb and forefinger. This mixes the fibers so that they bend and flair at random, forming a cylinder. Ascertain the desired length and tie in.

Wings can also be made from animal hair—from woodchuck to polar bear.

EMERGING SPRING MAYFLY

Wrap the shank with tying silk and tie in the brown carpet thread rib. Since it is the last body material to be used, it is the first to be tied in. Tie in body material, which should be as water absorbing as possible.

Body taper is made by wrapping more material in the center of the shank than at the ends.

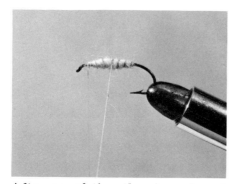

After completing the cigar-shaped body, clip excess body material and counter wrap in the opposite direction the brown carpet thread rib to strengthen the body.

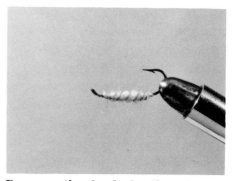

Reverse the hook in the vise so that the fly is belly up. It is much easier to attach beard-type hackle in this position.

Select a bunch of hackle beard from a partridge feather and tie in. The hackle should flair away from the body. Clip hackle butts and you are now ready for winging.

The method of hackling which I prefer for most of my wet flies is the full hackle. Begin by taking a partridge feather and stripping away the fuzz. Let one side be a little shorter than the other. Flatten the quill with thumb and forefinger and tie in. The shorter side of the feather should be in the direction you will be winding on the hackle. Clip excess quill.

Take a few turns of hackle and tie off. Exercise caution: it is easy to overdress with more turns than needed.

Select a pair of wings from a wild-fowl's flight quills and tie in down wing.

The most common hair wings are made from the common animals. These include gray, red, and black squirrels, deer and kip tails, skunk guard hair found along the back as well as the tail, etc. Using hair for wet-fly wings requires that the tier takes care when tying. The hair can slip if tension is not applied to the thread. How much tension? Almost as much as the thread can take without breaking. I also apply a drop of lacquer to the wing at the point where I'm tying, and then the tie over the lacquered hair. This bonds the tying thread under the hair; the hair and the anchoring wraps over the wing into one solid unit. It also keeps such wings from loosening and spinning about the shank.

Clip excess wing material, form head in usual manner, tie off, and lacquer.

Chenille is a good material for making wet-fly bodies. It comes in a variety of colors, ties easily, and absorbs water readily.

The rolled feather wing, tied in down-wing, is another popular wet-fly wing. The wing should be rolled between thumb and forefinger and tied in so that the wing tip extends at or slightly beyond the band of the hook.

The rolled feather wing acts as a unit when worked in the water.

Peacock fibers wound together as a single strand and strengthened by counter winding of tying thread makes for a natural body material similar to chenille. The peacock fibers pulsate as the fly is worked through the water.

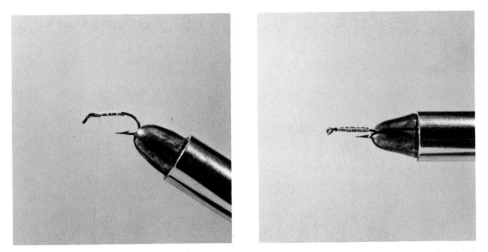

Wet flies can be weighted with lead wire to make them sink faster in fast
heavy water. A single strand can be tied in under the shank of the hook,
or on the sides of the shank if a flat body is wanted. If used in excess,
lead has a way of killing the action of the fly and disturbing the center
of gravity to the point where the fly works upside down.

Here is a typical wet-fly pattern with common dressing variations. Couple
this section with what was learned in the dry-fly chapter and you will be
well on your way to meeting local conditions head-on.

EMERGING SPRING MAYFLY

Tail:	None
Rib:	Heavy gray spun mohair
Body:	Light gray spun mohair
Hackle:	Grouse body feather (taken from the breast region of an adult male)
Wing:	Matching sections taken from left- and right-wing quills of a mallard duck

CHAPTER 5

THE NYMPH

Nymphs are among the easiest flies to make, yet the most difficult to fish correctly. Nymphs represent the aquatic stage in the life cycle of mayflies, stoneflies, and caddisflies. They develop from an egg deposited by the female in running water. The act of depositing can range from simply dropping the eggs from the air, bomber style, to the female diving down and depositing the eggs personally on rocks and underwater vegetation. They can be found in slow, quiet water running on a loamy bottom, or fast, boulder water running on a rocky bottom.

When one learns how to fish nymphs, it is one of the most consistently deadly means of taking trout known to man. In part this is due to the fact that nymphs represent the largest portion of the average trout's diet.

To be successful, the nymphing angler must be patient and methodical—like a fine quail dog whose specialty it is to hunt up singles after the covey has been dispersed. Or a New England grouse dog who is particularly gifted with the attributes for finding and being able to hold that artful dodger of the woods. Both have the same type of temperament the nymphing angler should have.

How does one draw that fine line which differentiates fishing the wet fly from the nymph? It is difficult, because so often the two techniques overlap. But, nailed to the wall for a definition, the basic differences between the two is how their live counterparts act in the water. I see the wet fly as the stage in the life cycle when the insect is undergoing a metamorphosis from nymph to dry fly. The insect is struggling to the surface where he can shed his underwater skin for which he no longer has any need. I call this a wet-fly action. The nymph, on the other hand, is much more dependent upon the currents of his habitat. In quiet water the nymph swims almost effortlessly. Some species swim in a jerky uneven motion while others move through the water smoothly. All of the foregoing is dependent upon the individual species. It is for this reason that a fly tier must be inquisitive if he is going to produce taking lures. Very often, how the lures are fished go hand in hand with the fly itself.

The nymph can be fished across and downstream or upstream on a dead or near-dead drift. If worked across and down, care should be taken to match the lure's action to the natural you are trying to imitate. The action of the rod comes into play here as you work the line. A little wrist action of the rod hand goes a long way in producing just the right amount of twitch.

Regardless of which casting method is employed, the angler should be sweeping all possible resting and feeding stations if top results are to be obtained. Fishing up or downstream, the fly should arrive at the preselected spot at the right height above the bottom. You can regulate the fly depth desired by the placing of your fly in the currents to take a fly deep. Less of an upstream cast will shallow the lure's depth.

As the nymph begins to move through the area you want to fish, raise your rod tip gently. And, I mean gently. Too fast or jerky a movement will telegraph fraud to the fish, and give you away. When the fly has moved between eight and twelve inches, perform a slight twitch by taking up a few inches of line. If you have guessed right, hang on for a smashing strike.

In my angling career, I have had few, if any, strikes which I can truly call soft. For the most part, they have been of the bone-jarring variety. A soft strike occurs when you lay a fly directly to a fish and he doesn't have to move to take it. His action of moving water over his gills is enough to suck in the fly. If he doesn't hook himself, and the odds are that he won't, he'll just spit out the fraud. With the soft underwater take, the angler must impart the hooking action.

I have had fish move great distances to take a fly. Often, I didn't see the take myself but others later related it to me. When a fish moves to take a fly, even if it is only a few feet, he is going to nail it, by hitting it hard. If the fish hits a lure, his swimming momentum alone will almost cause him to hook himself.

I'm glad that I don't fish where the soft strikes of other angling writers are common. Such antics would drive me to distraction.

When fishing quiet still waters, as little action as possible should be imparted to your fly. If necessary, use a sinking line or an undressed floating line. Both can be used, depending upon the depth desired; both will sink the fly and leader. I am of the opinion that in clear water fish can see great distances. If the action of the fly is right, they will move great distances to take an appealing fly. Fishing nymphs does take a bit more effort than some other methods of angling, but it is not that difficult to master. It does mean, however, that to be successful you're going to have to be a bit more alert and perceptive to your surroundings. However, I think this adds enjoyment to the game.

Fishing nymphs takes just as much casting finesse as the dry fly. If you know where the fish usually congregate in any particular section of water, then make your first cast directly to this spot. Otherwise, start with a short cast until you have covered the entire piece of water or find the fish.

Where the long cast is necessary because the fish is able to realize your presence or you're afraid of spooking him, your approach should be made with great care. If the stream is small or a bit on the shallow side, get on your knees if necessary and make your first cast from some distance below, allowing the nymph to alight on the water at the tail end of the pool. If there is fast water below the pool, making such a cast unfeasible, then work up to the pool with as little disturbance as you can and wait there for the time necessary before making your next cast.

After the cast has been completed, the nymph should immediately sink, and it is allowed to descend until it almost reaches the bottom. Care should be taken that the fly doesn't reach bottom. It is easy to get hung up on the bottom. If this happens, you will spook your quarry for sure. As the nymph descends, watch your line for any movement not in keeping with the normal sinking process. Should it jerk slightly or suddenly straighten out after it has started to curve, be prepared to set the hook without delay. Keep slack line to a minimum. If the fish is moving when he takes the fly, and the line has little slack, the fish will require little setting of the hook. He will almost set it himself. If nothing occurs or if you miss the strike, let the fly move a bit

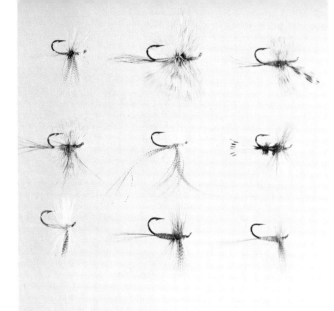

DRY FLIES

Hendrickson E. B. D.

Wing   Mandarin or wood duck flank feather
Body   Pink fur from red fox vixen (urine burned)
Hackle   Light blue dun
Tail   Light blue dun

Dark Cahill E. B. D.

Wing   Mandarin or wood duck flank feather
Body   Gray fox or muskrat
Hackle   Brown
Tail   Brown

Light Cahill E. B. D.

Wing   Mandarin or wood duck flank feather
Body   Light red fox belly fur
Hackle   Light ginger
Tail   Light ginger

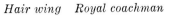

Hair wing   Royal coachman

Wing   Calf tail
Body   Peacock herl and scarlet floss
Hackle   Brown
Tail   Golden pheasant tippet

Two-Feathered Fly

Body, tail, and wing   From same unbroken mandarin
                                 or wood duck flank feather
Hackle   Light ginger

Gold's Egg-sack

Wing   Deer hair (dark)
Body   Gray fox and beaver mixed one to one
Egg sack   Greenish gold wool
Tail   Deer hair (dark)
Hackle   Grizzly

Gray Stone Fly

Wing   Grizzly hackle points
Body   Gray muskrat
Hackle   Grizzly and brown mixed
Tail   Grizzly and brown mixed

Salmon Fly

Wing   Two pairs of bastard grizzly
Body   Fluorescent orange floss
Hackle   Grizzly and ginger mixed
Tail   Woodchuck

Quill Gordon

Wing   Mandarin or wood duck flank feather
Body   Stripped quill from peacock eye feather
Hackle   Dun
Tail   Dun

Hewitt's Skater H. A. D.
Large dun saddle hackle
Guinea hen

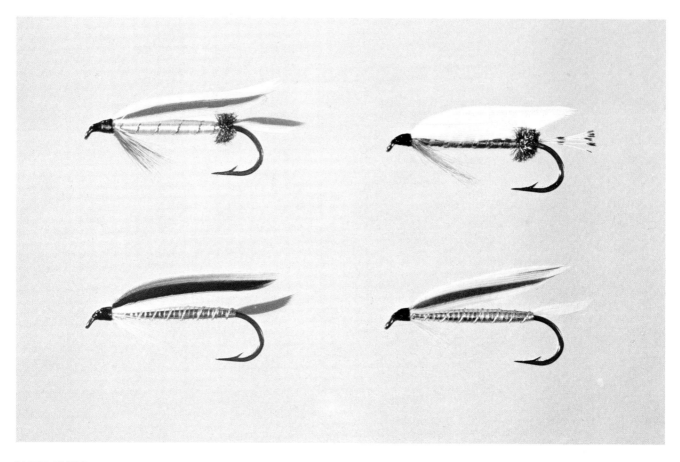

WET FLIES

Parmachene Bell C. K.

Wing   Red, white, and red primary wing quill sections
          married together
Body   Yellow floss
Rib   Oval silver tinsel
Egg Sac   Peacock herl
Hackle   Red hackle
Tail   Red and white quill sections married

Royal Coachman C. K.

Wing   White goose quill primary sections
Body   Scarlet floss
Rib   Flat silver tinsel
Egg Sac   Peacock herl
Hackle   Brown
Tail   Golden pheasant tippets

Jesse Wood C. K.

Wing   Brown, black, and white primary wing sections
          married together
Body   Flat silver tinsel
Rib   Oval silver tinsel
Hackle   White
Tail   Red primary wing quill section

Colonel Fuller C. K.

Wing   Yellow, red, and yellow primary wing quill
          sections married together
Body   Flat silver tinsel
Rib   Oval silver tinsel
Hackle   Yellow
Tail   Yellow primary wing quill section

NYMPHS

Krom March Brown Nymph

See page 71.

Green Drake Nymph C. K.

Body   White fur
Rib   White ostrich herl
Gills   White ostrich herl
Wing Case   Brown partridge
Legs   Gray partridge
Tails   Three brown hackle quills
Head   Brown

Krom Stone Fly

See page 66.

Large Brown Stone Fly Nymph

See page 74.

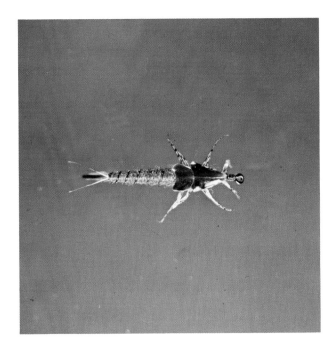

STREAMER FLIES

Silver Tip Bucktail C. K.

Body   Four to six strands of fine gold oval tinsel, tied
        in together
Wing   Silver tip grizzly bear hair
Tail   Red wool
Cheeks Jungle cock
Head   Black with a fine red ring at the base

Ghost Shiner C. K.

Body   White floss
Rib   Flat silver tinsel
Wing   Light tan summer sable
Tail   Light green floss
Cheeks Jungle cock
Hackle White
Head   Gray

Royal Coachman C. K.

Body   Scarlet floss
Rib   Flat silver tinsel
Wing   White saddle hackle
Tail   Red primary wing quill
Cheeks Jungle cock
Hackle Brown
Egg Sac Peacock herl

Hell's Angel C. K.

Body   Flat silver tinsel
Wing   Black and orange bucktail
Cheeks Jungle cock
Hackle Red

Shushan Postmaster Bucktail K. F.

Body   Light yellow floss
Rib   Flat gold tinsel
Wing   Fox squirrel tail hair
Tail   Mottled brown turkey feather
Cheeks Jungle cock
Hackle Dyed red duck quill

Black Ghost Streamer K. F.

Body   Black floss
Rib   Flat silver
Wing   White saddle hackles
Tail   Yellow saddle hackle
Cheeks Jungle cock
Hackle Yellow saddle hackle

SALMON FLIES

Rat-Faced McDougall

See page 98.

Defeo's Gold Mongrel C. K.

Tag   Oval gold tinsel
Sac   Fluorescent orange floss
Butt   Peacock herl
Tail   Brown hackle
Body   Flat gold tinsel
Rib   Oval gold tinsel
Hackle   Brown hen hackle
Wing   Red hair of baboon skin
Head   Black silk

Red Abbey

Tag   Oval silver tinsel
Tail   Golden pheasant crest
Body   Red floss
Rib   Flat silver tinsel
Hackle   Yellow
Wing   Fox squirrel tail
Head   Black

Copper Killer

Tag   A few turns of copper wire
Tip   Pale green floss, small
Tail   Fox squirrel tail hair
Butt   Bright red floss, small
Body   Flat copper tinsel
Ribbing   Round copper wire or oval copper tinsel
Hackle   Bright orange
Wing   Fox squirrel tail hair

Nepissequit Gray

Tag   Oval gold tinsel
Sac   Yellow silk
Butt   Peacock herl
Tail   Golden pheasant crest
Body   Gray muskrat
Rib   Oval gold tinsel
Hackle   Black or grizzly hen
Wing   Black bear hair
Head   Black silk

Rusty Rat

Tag   Oval gold tinsel
Tail   Three peacock sword fibers
Body   Rear half, yellow gold floss; forward half, peacock herl
Rib   Oval gold tinsel
Wing   Gray fox guard hairs
Hackle   Grizzly

Chief Needabeh

Tag   Flat silver tinsel
Body   Scarlet floss
Rib   Flat silver floss
Wing   Two yellow and two red saddle hackle fibers
Hackle   Red hackle
Cheeks   Jungle cock
Head   Black

De Feo's Salmon Nymphs

Black Nymph

Tag   Fine flat gold tinsel
Tip   Orange floss
Tail   Three brown mallard fibers
Butt   Peacock herl
Body   Black seal's fur
Throat   Mallard fibers
Wing   Small jungle cock hackle tip tied flat

Silver Nymph

Tag   Fine flat silver tinsel
Tip   Orange floss
Tail   Three brown mallard fibers
Butt   Peacock herl
Body   Rear half, oval silver tinsel; front half, peacock
        herl
Throat   Mallard fibers
Wing   Small jungle cock hackle tip tied flat

Gold Nymph

Tag   Fine flat silver tinsel
Tip   Orange floss
Tail   Three brown mallard fibers
Butt   Peacock herl
Body   Rear half, oval gold tinsel; front half, peacock
        herl
Throat   Mallard fibers
Wing   Small jungle cock hackle tip tied flat

De Feo's Beaver Nymph

Tail   Two beaver guard hairs
Body   Unstripped eye quill from peacock tail feather
Legs   Beaver guard hairs
Head   Red

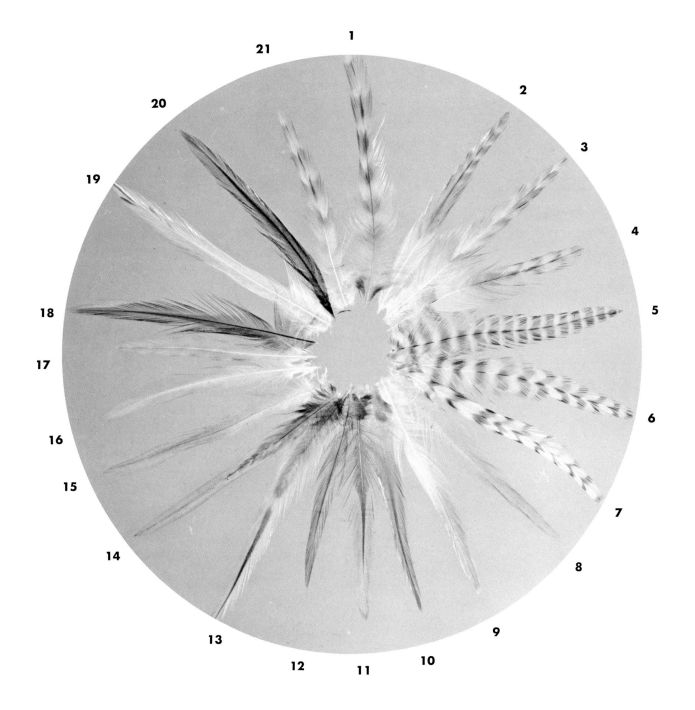

NATURALS

Hackle Color Chart

1. Natural red
2. Furnace
3. Dark honey dun
4. Honey dun
5. Light honey dun
6. Light blue dun
7. Barred dun
8. Dark blue dun
9. White
10. Black
11. Red grizzly
12. Dark grizzly
13. Light bastard (barred plymouth rock and red grizzly mix)
14. Dark bastard
15. Light plymouth rock
16. Medium plymouth rock
17. Dark plymouth rock
18. Dark ginger
19. Light ginger
20. Brown
21. Cochy-bondhu

further before starting a slow, hand retrieve made by taking in a few inches of line at a time. The speed of the retrieve should be governed by the fly you have on, the natural's action you are trying to imitate, and the speed of the current's flow. Sometimes it is best to let the nymph rest in the flow after your line has straightened out before beginning to retrieve. A few twitches make a fish take after the nymph has rested and before being retrieved. When beginning the retrieve, lift the rod so that is it between 45 and 60 degrees with the water. This lifting of the rod tip starts the fly moving toward the surface. Another trick is to drop the rod tip or bob it, imparting life to the lure.

After locating a spot which produces for you, fish it with care. Retrieve the lure until you can lift it from the water without making a disturbance. A sloppy lift from the water will quite often spoil the chances of taking any more fish. If your fly should land in the wrong place, finish the cast; don't lift the fly from the surface at once. Your chances of taking fish with your fly in the air is exceedingly slim. Fish your miscast just as if it went to the very place you intended it to go. Take your time between casts; haste has a way of making the situation into a disaster. If you are careful, you will take far more fish than you could by racing along the stream trying to fish in as many spots as possible.

Nymphs, like other types of flies, should be made to fit individual water conditions. Shallow, slow-moving streams require a lighter lure than one designed to fish fast, heavy water. To control the sinking rate of your lures, match the hook's wire size to meet these conditions. I tie my lures on hooks ranging from standard fine-wire hooks (used on dry flies) to those having extra heavy wire. When I want even more weight, I add lead wire. It's available in several diameters from which to choose. I would like to caution the overuse of lead wire, however. You can make your fly heavier than need be and do away with its action. Given a choice, I would rather have my own flies lighter rather than heavier than need be.

The successful tying and designing of nymphs is greatly dependent upon the maker's ability to invent, use new and different materials, and employ creative tying techniques to bring life to them. By the time a new tying angler reaches the stage where he is fishing the nymph, he is usually ready to begin experimentation, to start innovating his own patterns to meet local conditions.

When it comes to tying nymphs, Charles Krom can be considered a master at his craft. He is an innovator in the truest sense. Not only does he utilize new materials and techniques to their fullest potential, he develops new patterns as well. And the patterns which Krom develops are consistent in taking trout. Never content, he constantly strives to improve and surpass previous efforts.

THE KROM STONEFLY NYMPH

Tail: Two peccary fibers
Underbody: White silk floss
Body: Two eye quills, which have been stripped, taken from a peacock tail feather
Abdomen: Four strands of peacock herl, twisted together to form a single strand
Legs: Brown hackle
Wing Covert: Chocolate-brown secondary wing quills taken from a mallard duck. Each duck usually has two or three such colored quills.
Thread: Dark-brown silk

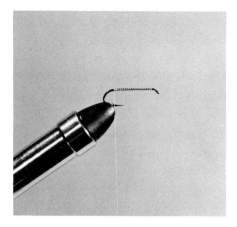

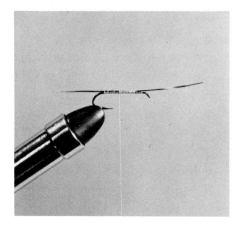

Wrap the shank of the hook with tying silk to the point above the barb. The silk-wrapped shank provides a solid base necessary to support the materials to be tied in.

Tie in two peccary fibers for the tails. The length of the tails are governed by the length of the nymph's body. Both are equal in length.

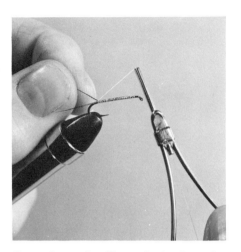

With a dubbing needle separate the two tail fibers at the point on the shank where they are wrapped. Clip excess butt material.

Spread each fiber forty-five degrees to the shank and anchor into position with tying silk.

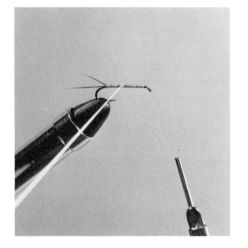

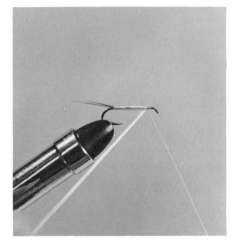

Tie in the white silk floss underbody midway on the hook's shank. At this point, the body diameter will be the widest. When wrapping the floss, care should be taken not to make the tapered cigar-shaped body too heavy.

Tie off the silk-floss underbody at a point which will leave enough working room behind the head for the other tying stages and return the tying thread to the point where the tail meets the body.

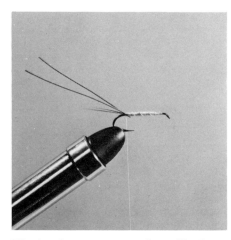

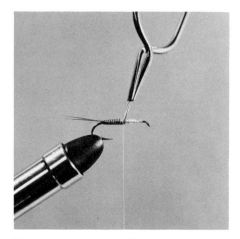

Tie in the two peacock quill fibers at the point where the body joins the tails. Note that each quill has a dark- and light-colored edge.

Face the two quills so that the light edge overlaps the dark, and wrap the quills together over one-half the length of the floss under-body. Tie off the quills with several turns of tying silk.

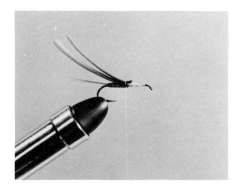

Tie in a single palmered brown hackle, which is to simulate the nymph's legs. Note that the materials which emanate from a single point are tied in such that their order of use is reversed. The wing covert is tied in first, but is used last.

Tie in the mallard chocolate-colored secondary wing fiber sections by the heavy butt ends. The fibers should be tied in on each side of the top of the shank, over-lapping at the center. A realistic wing case can't be made easily from one bunch of fibers.

Tie in three or four strands of peacock herl. Twist the strands to make a single working thread. For added strength, spiral tying thread in the opposite direction to the lay of the twisted herl. The stronger thread keeps the herl from being cut by the fish's teeth.

Wind on the herl to form the nymph's thorax. Note that there is still room behind the eye for other materials to be tied in. Tie off the herl.

Form the nymph's legs by winding the palmered brown hackle over the peacock thorax. This too is done against the lay of the wraps of herl. Tie off the hackle.

With the dubbing needle, spread the brown hackle fibers to each side of the thorax. When the wing case is tied into position, it will keep the fibers from springing back into their upright position.

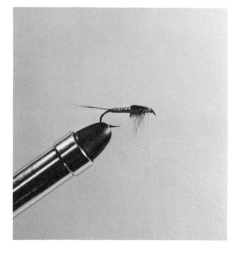

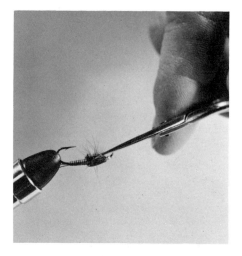

Bring the wing covert over the forced-down hackle fibers and tie off at the base of the head. Clip off the excess covert material and form the head from tying silk. Use the whip finish to complete the small neat head.

Flip the fly over on its back and clip the center portion of hackle underneath the body to form realistic legs.

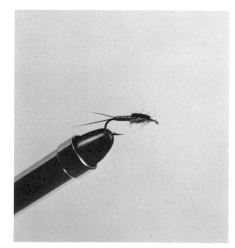

Give the head several coats of lacquer, letting each coat dry before applying the next, to build a realistic, glossy surfaced head. Your fly is now ready for the stream.

Several years ago, Charles developed a beautiful March Brown Nymph. It proved to be a successful fly, and rapidly gained a reputation for taking trout on a regular basis. From Charles' point of view, it developed one flaw, a flaw which was to bring about a whole new approach to tying fly bodies. Because the weakness of the March Brown was not in the way it was tied or its ability to dupe trout, most originators and tiers would have stopped there. It is to his credit that he did not.

The March Brown's major fault as Charles viewed it was that the abdomen was made from the fiber of a condor's wing quill. Condors are one of the species of birds now on the endangered list. He felt so strongly about wanting to protect this bird that he began exploring other methods of making quill bodies. He found the ideal solution in utilizing the many easily obtainable colors of cotton sewing thread. Here then is the new Krom March Brown Nymph—with strands of different colored cotton thread used to bring out the segmented body effect. The thread is lacquered with several coats to allow the colors to become bright.

THE KROM MARCH BROWN NYMPH

Tail: Three reddish-brown fibers taken from a mature cock pheasant center tail feather

Abdomen: One amber and two light-olive strands of cotton thread waxed and wound together over white floss underbody. Lacquer several times to bring out color. Take care to let each coat dry before applying the next.

Thorax: Light beaver fur

Wing Case: Cinnamon turkey

Legs: Grizzly and brown hackle wound on together

Head: Brown tying thread

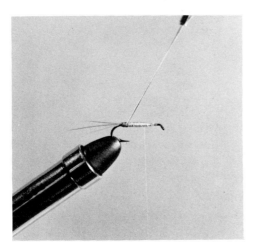

Wrap the shank of the hook as described in the Krom Stone Fly. Tie in the fibers for the tails. Since there are three tails, the center one extends beyond the body while the outside fibers extend at a forty-five-degree angle to the hook's shank. Tie in white silk floss underbody as in the Krom Stone Fly. Next, tie in one amber and two light olive strands of cotton thread to form abdomen and wind on over the white floss underbody to form natural segments.

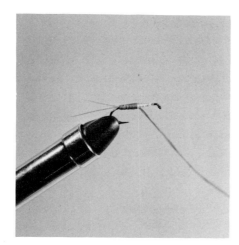

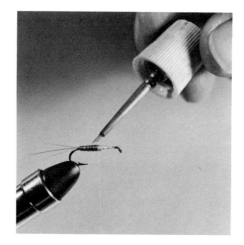

Tie off cotton thread strands and clip excess. The abdomen should extend just beyond the widest diameter of the cigar-shaped underbody.

Apply several coats of lacquer to the thread abdomen, letting each coat dry before applying the next. This makes for a more natural looking abdomen and prevents fish from cutting strands.

Tie in two sections from a cinnamon turkey wing quill to form wing case. Then tie in one each brown and grizzly hackles. Prepare light brown or tan beaver fur dubbing.

Wind on dubbing to form thorax. The dubbing should be tapered to form a natural looking silhouetted lure.

Both the grizzly and brown hackles are tied around the dubbed thorax together. If done separately, the color effect is completely different.

Bend the hackle fibers to the sides and lay over the turkey feather wing case. Tie on and clip excess material. Form head and complete with whip finish. As in the Krom Stone Fly, invert the fly in the vise and clip the center portion of the hackle to form legs.

Apply several coats of lacquer to the head, and you're ready to go fishing. Note that the tail is about one and one-half times as long as the body.

LARGE BROWN STONEFLY NYMPH

Tail: Brown tipped peccary with white segments
Body: Brown worsted wool or beaver fur
Rib: Heavy-diameter monofilament which has been dyed a rich
                 brown
Thorax:
Legs: Grouse body feather
Wing Case: Two mottled grouse feathers lacquered and trimmed to
                 shape
Hook: Mustad No. 3665A streamer hook

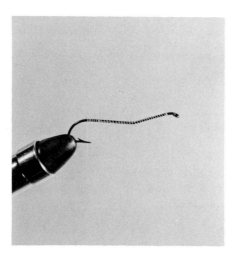

Bend hook with a pair of pliers and wrap shank to prepare under-body.

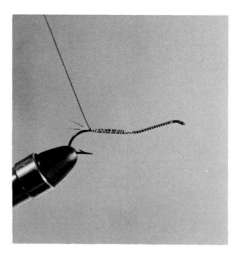

Tie in the two peccary tail fibers so that the white is showing. They should be short, extending just beyond the end of the hook. The two fibers should be spread thirty degrees from the shank of the hook. After the tail has been set, tie in the rich brown monofilament rib.

Tie in, wrap, and shape the abdomen with worsted wool. If wool is unavailable, use dark brown beaver dubbing. Tie wool off at segment between abdomen and thorax to form natural looking body.

Shape thorax with body material and tie off behind head. Leave enough room behind the eye for other materials to be tied in. Apply cement to the thorax which holds the legs.

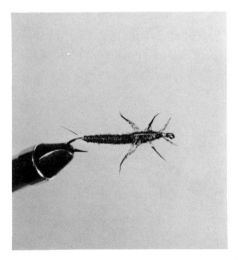

Tie in a single grouse body feather to make the legs. Each leg is made from grouped fibers cemented together with lacquer.

Strip away the unwanted fuzz from two mottled grouse body feathers. Lacquer the surfaces and trim to shape when dry.

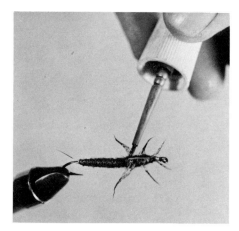

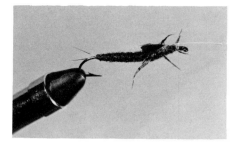

Place each of the two prepared grouse feathers individually on the glued thorax and tie in.

Apply glue to the center portion of the thorax, covering the quill which forms the legs.

The wing case should extend the length of the thorax. Form the head, with dark brown tying thread, and lacquer with several coats until glossy.

∧∧∧∧∧ CHAPTER 6 ∧∧∧∧∧

STREAMERS AND BUCKTAILS

By nature I am an angler who enjoys fishing streamers and I will only switch to other methods when conditions dictate a change. This is not often. I believe fish take such large flies because they mistake them for minnows or large nymphs. I have learned that big flies usually mean big fish. It may also mean fewer fish. Other angling methods generally yield smaller fish.

It would be foolish for me to say that angling (trout fishing in particular) follows any given rule. There are too many variables, and no way of cataloguing them to fit specific circumstances. Because of this, angling remains the most fascinating of all sports. The deeply mysterious and subtle changes which occur on the stream from day to day during the angler's season are reason enough for the many theories and methods which have become such a part of the sport.

It must be recognized by anyone who has ever cast a fly that there is no fixed rule in presenting, methods of pattern selection, or making imitations. To better understand the trout's world, it must be realized that the stream is not a flowing conduit pipe containing water, various and sundry chemicals, and perhaps a few fish, but rather an individual, smaller, yet separate environment within and part of a larger more encompassing framework. This smaller and sustaining environment contains fish which are only one link in a long chain of life. To support trout, a stream must have a balance of food, oxygenated water within the correct acidity and alkalinity limits, and shelter conditions which encourage plant and animal life and growth within. If the blend is correct, a kaleidoscopic picture is formed, reflecting itself in the many moods of the trout. Of the many miles of stream probed by the angler's fly, no two pools are ever the same, no two runs alike in form, depth, or flow. They remain a challenge to the angler's imagination and adaptability.

It is for this reason that, given a choice, I prefer large streams, full wide rivers that one can never hope to understand. For here it becomes impossible to achieve a close intimately physical understanding of all the deep runs and dark holes. Seldom is it possible on a large piece of water to sit quietly on the bank, watching the movement of caddisflies and mayflies, the creeping emergence of stoneflies, the finning of a resting trout, or the silver flash of a taking fish. Big water conceals all this. To me, it becomes more exciting.

Small water on the other hand is ideal for learning. It teaches the trout's habits and habitat. Don't delude yourself into thinking that large trout only inhabit big water. They can be found in small brushy streams, and offer a challenge that big-water trout can't give. It is an old axiom that big trout didn't get big by being gullible enough to fall for every lure that came floating by. Usually such fish have adequate protection and food supply.

I recall a beautiful two-and-a-half-pound brown that lived below bank in a vacated muskrat hole. The currents were such that food came almost to his door. He ruled the pool. There were few smaller fish to be found there. What minnows there were, stayed well in the shallows for protection. Because of the small size of the stream, and the overhanging foliage, casting was a problem. Usually, because of the brush, one spooked him for the day by the time one worked into casting position.

I learned a lot from that fish. It took me almost a full season to get onto him. Because of the lack of minnows and small fish, I felt that he would go first for a streamer. But how to get it to him was the problem. In all previous casts I had stood above him, trying to get the fly to him by casting down and across. No luck at all. Finally it dawned on me to try him from below. This was the ticket. On the first cast upstream I put the fly above him, as I would a dry fly. A slight tap on the line put the fly at the right depth. I let the currents do their work, and, when the fly was within his vision range, a few twitches of the line was all it took to fool him. Had I continued as I had begun and as had everyone else, he would have remained uncaught. As I said, big trout didn't get big by being stupid.

Of all the artificials conceived of miscellaneous fur and feathers, these big flies are best adapted for big water and larger trout. Surely, the deadly effect of these flies cannot be denied when conditions are right.

Bucktails and streamers are ideal for early spring fishing. Insect activity is not great enough to attract the larger fishes' attention. If bucktails and streamers imitate minnows, let them be as large as minnows. When does a minnow cease being a minnow? That I'll leave to your own conclusions.

Most anglers stop using the streamer as soon as the spring high-water levels start to recede. This, I think, is a mistake. I have had good luck with the streamer all through the season. I have even made such flies on fine-wire hooks. Such light-wire streamers and bucktails have proved very successful the latter half of the season. By the way, in the latter half of the season there are not nearly as many anglers on the stream as during the first half. And, in my opinion, the angling improves.

Probably the strangest thing about fishing such flies is their ability to raise a really big fish a successive number of times until the hook finally takes. I know no other lure type of which I can say the same. A trout coming short to the other types of flies is difficult to get to take again, even after a long rest. Bucktails, however, excite fish to the point of wreckless abandonment; and they will come again and again unless frightened or spooked, until hooked.

An incident which proves this point stands out in my mind. I first became interested in streamers and this type of angling through my association with Keith Fulsher. Keith is the originator of the Thunder Creek Bait Fish Imitation Series. These flies are tied on ring-eyed hooks for the most part. They have a unique head and a wing which ends just aft of the hook's bend which makes them more appealing. I thought longer-winged flies looked and fished better. I made some and tried them out. I began missing strikes. It finally dawned on me that the cause was the too-long wing. I clipped some of the wing off, went back to my last fish, and cast to him again. He struck short

THUNDER CREEK SERIES OF BAIT FISH IMITATIONS

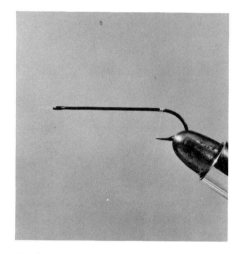

Begin any of the Thunder Creek series by taking a few turns of thread about the shank at the barb.

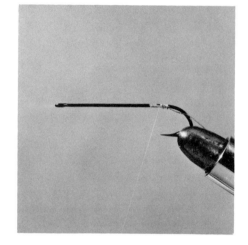

Silver Shiner calls for an oval rib. Since the rib is wrapped over the flat tinsel body, it is tied in first.

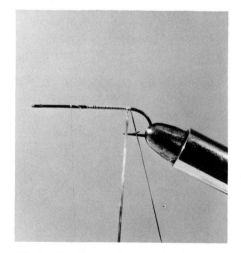

Tie in the flat body tinsel and wind the tying thread about the shank to the point where the body will end.

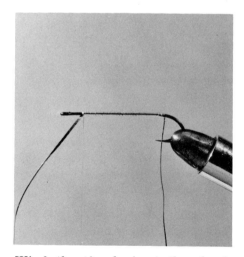

Wind the tinsel about the shank to form the body. The tinsel should lay edge to edge, flat and without gaps.

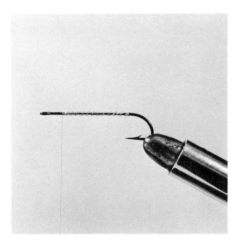

Counter-wind the tinsel rib.

Select a bunch of brown bucktail fibers. Adjust their tips so that they are even and tie in. The fibers should not be allowed to rotate but be confined to the top half of the shank.

Apply a drop of glue to the hair at the thread and tie forward to the point where the eye begins. Clip the unwanted butts and apply another drop of lacquer.

Reverse the hook in the vise and repeat the procedure using white bucktail fibers for the belly. The white and brown fibers should be the same length.

Stroke the fibers so that they begin to lay back with little effort. At this time, all short fibers should be removed.

Grasp the hair as firmly as possible without breaking, and take several turns with thread to form the gills and head. If done correctly, there should be a line of distinction between the light and dark fibers. Tie off with the whip finishing knot.

Apply several coats of lacquer to the head, letting lacquer dry between coats. When the lacquer has been built up to form a smooth head, apply a black dot to form the background for the eye.

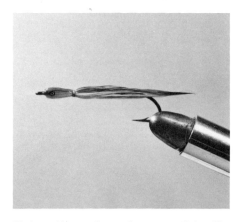

Using the point of a round toothpick, make a small yellow dot in the center of the black. Let dry and apply one more coat of clear lacquer over the entire head. Your fly is now complete.

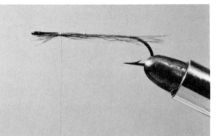

If a stripe is desired, which will run down the median line of the lure, attach appropriate colored fibers prior to tying in the brown or white fibers.

If an underwing is wanted, prepare it prior to tying in the brown or white bucktail fibers.

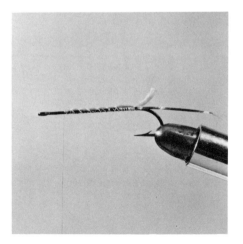

If a tail is wanted, tie it in prior to winding on the tinsel body. To avoid a lump at the base of the tail, extend the tail material the full length of the body and wrap the body material over it.

again. I shortened the wing some more. This went on until I finally caught the fish. I learned in one lesson and rather quickly that Keith Fulsher knows how long to make his wings.

The success of the streamer is due in large part to the fact that the bigger a fish gets, the more food he requires. He reaches a point where his food intake is greater than what he can obtain by just eating insects. He turns to minnows, large nymphs, frogs, small newborn ducklings, and mice. Likewise, when the heavy rains begin to fall, they bring a roil of mud which covers the feeding movement of big fish. Fish move out to feed on the incoming bonanza of new food—much of it in the form of night crawlers, grubs, and other terrestrial insects.

There are a few pointers which will aid you in tying and fishing streamers. By far the most important is the fact that overdressing wings can kill the streamer's action. *Sparse* is the word. As I mentioned earlier, wings should also be on the short side after passing the bend of the hook. When using bucktail and simliar-type animals tails, care should be taken to select only those having fine strands. This can be a problem at times. The longer hair suitable for tying larger streamers comes from older animals. Older animals also have coarser hair.

With regard to hackle used for wings, choose the soft saddle hackles. By soft, I mean those feathers having a soft pliable stem and fibers containing some web. Such feathers will work better in the water. Stay away from the large neck hackle fibers if you can help it. They are usually too stiff to be effective in all but accelerated currents.

I prefer my streamers to be a bit on the large size. However, if a particular situation calls for a miniature tied on a 3X-long shank standard or even on an extra-fine-wire hook, I have no compulsion against making and using them that small.

Only a few patterns are necessary. I use both the feather and hackle wing types. If large enough body feathers can be found, I'll make rolled wings. However, finding large enough feathers is always a problem.

THE BLACK GHOST STREAMER

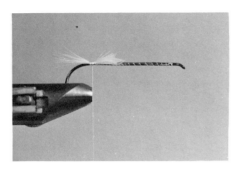

Take a bunch of yellow hackle fibers and tie them in for the tail. Clip excess butt material.

Tie in the flat silver rib and the black floss body material. Taper the body.

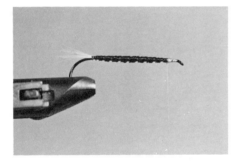

Wrap the silver tinsel to form the rib, wrapping as tightly as possible so that it doesn't slip.

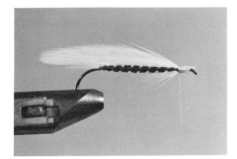

Tie in a hackle beard of yellow fibers from the same feather as the tail. Match a pair of white saddle hackles and tie in.

Add a cheek to each side, form the head, and apply several coats of lacquer to finish the fly.

SUSHAN POSTMASTER

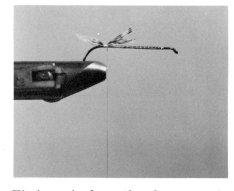

Tie in a single section from a mottled turkey quill for the tail. Trim excess butt material.

Tie in some flat gold tinsel just forward of the tail. Work the tying silk to the body mid-point and tie in the gold floss.

Build a tapered body, making the thickest part where the floss was tied in. With the body complete, wrap the tinsel rib.

Take a small portion of tied red duck quill and form a beard with it. Note how the quill fibers flair away from the body.

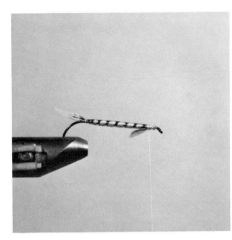

Trim excess red quill and take several turns of thread to form a solid base for the hair.

Select a portion of red squirrel tail, even the ends, and tie in.

Clip excess hair, add some cheeks, and form the head. Apply several coats of lacquer to finish the fly.

⋀⋀⋀⋀⋀⋀ CHAPTER 7 ⋀⋀⋀⋀⋀⋀

THE SALMON FLY

Atlantic salmon are a paradox. It's almost inconceivable that a fish which is not feeding and that has little or no food in its stomach will take an angler's fly. If this is so (and it is), then why do they? Even stranger still is the angler who seeks such non-feeding fish.

The question of why a salmon takes a fly has never really been solved. The answer which seems to hold the greatest validity and promise is that the fish take a fly out of habit. It is a conditioned response. This response first began when the salmon used up what food was left in their yolk sacs and were forced to seek food from their environment. As parr, they fed on all available river foodstuffs. This included water, land, and flying insects as well as minnows. This conditioning process of having to search for their own food continued and grew when they migrated and lived in the sea. As grilse, on their first spawning run back to the river, the need for food diminishes and finally stops. The biological built-in response after food recognition takes place still exists. Thus, upon recognizing food, the salmon is conditioned to respond by taking, even though he has no need for the food. It is this preconditioning of feeding which overpowers the delicate biological balance of his mating instincts.

Salmon will not just confine their feeding habits to subsurface lures and food. They will take surface and flying insects as well. Countless reports have been verified which state that salmon were seen taking insects flying above the surface.

The materials from which salmon flies are made are an excellent example of materials being used to their best advantage. In about 1900, when salmon fishing became popular and English, Scotch, and Irish tiers made flies for their rivers, they made them fancy. And with good reason. First, fancy prices could not have been charged for plain-looking flies. Just as important, the breeding of ornamental fowl was a common hobby and pastime. Thus, the use of silver and golden pheasant and similar bright-colored natural feathers which could be bred and raised easily at home came into use.

Importation became another important source of feathers. It must be remembered that safaris and long trips to foreign countries such as India, Africa, and China were the province of the wealthy. Only the wealthy fished and still fish for European salmon. This same fashionability of travel overflowed to this country. After his presidency Teddy Roosevelt went on two safaris. His first lasted more than a year. It was to Africa to hunt and collect native big-game specimens for natural history museums. His second trip was to Brazil, where he explored parts of the Amazon River and its basin. If a traveler were a fisherman it was almost certain that a few "exotic" bird and animal skins would be brought home for him to have made into flies.

In Canada, where most North Americans do most of their Atlantic salmon fishing, most salmon flies were of the European variety. There were very few tiers of such flies, most of which were imported. Fancy feathers and furs were almost impossible to obtain. When they could be imported, prices were prohibitive. It was only natural then for local anglers and, in particular, fishing guides who were men of the river to begin developing their own successful patterns. These guides could not afford expensive imported materials. Most hunted native game to augment their food supply, and so they began to use native materials which were easily found in the area. For the most part, the flies that these men developed reflected the makers themselves. They were rugged, plain, no-nonsense types of flies. In the water they took fish better than their imported brethren. American salmon anglers are responsible for fostering new patterns and helping to develop what are currently known as the "Guide Patterns."

In the last few years, these Canadian Guide Patterns have been gaining in popularity on European rivers. They must be proving quite effective. They are certainly easier to tie than the fancy patterns. The only problem so far encountered is being able to find materials large enough to accommodate some of the larger size hooks used there.

Among the many different guide patterns which have been originated over the years, certain ones which the fish seem to favor have been noted. To add further variety, the style, size, and how the fly is tied are just as important as the pattern itself.

Spring fishing or fishing when the rivers are high roily and in a state of flood call for large flies if one is to take any fish at all. Large patterns are needed to attract attention. Besides the poor visibility, sticks and debris with which the fly must compete are being washed downstream in the currents. Such large flies are usually tied on large hooks. The large hooks also add much needed and desired weight for fast sinking and better action in the fast, heavy currents. In such water, bigger flies can be seen further and worked where the fish are laying. If you are in such a situation, and your guide can't be of help in securing the heavy flies needed, try contacting a local tackle shop. Seek out their advice. What is a new set of circumstances to you, is old hat to them. They are up on all the latest local news and information. Usually, they know who's taking fish, how many were caught, and the most taking flies being used. If you don't have materials to duplicate patterns being used, they can usually oblige or have a local tier make a few for you fast.

On most Canadian rivers, under normal conditions and water levels, flies tied on size four through eight hooks will usually be more than adequate. When the waters you are fishing are low, and the currents have all but disappeared, size ten and twelve hooks are the ones to be using. In short, the salmon angler should have a well-rounded kit to meet all water conditions with a variety of patterns and sizes.

RUSTY RAT
AND
DARK MYSTRY SALMON FLIES

These two flies represent typical Canadian Guide Pattern salmon flies. For the tier who is now accomplished in tying trout patterns, these flies should offer somewhat of a new challenge. The materials used in these flies are fewer than those contained in Irish, Scotch, and English patterns. But take special note, however, of the way these materials are used. Techniques differ somewhat from the avearge trout pattern.

RUSTY RAT

Tag: Oval gold tinsel
Butt: None
Tail: Peacock fibers (taken from body rather than tail feather)
Body: Front half—peacock herl taken from tail feather; back half—
          yellowish orange floss
Rib: Oval gold tinsel
Wing: Guard hairs from mature gray fox
Head: Black

DARK MYSTRY

Tag: Oval gold tinsel
Sac: Fluorescent orange floss
Butt: Black ostrich herl
Tail: Blue dun hen hackle fibers
Body: Tan floss
Rib: Oval gold tinsel
Hackle: Three wisps of guinea hen hackle fibers on each side
Wing: Turkey wing sections over strands of orange and red fluores-
          cent floss
Head: Black

RUSTY RAT SALMON FLY

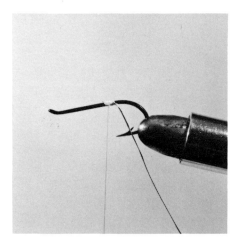

Place a standard or low-water, up-eyed salmon hook in your vise. Wrap a base of tying thread and tie in a piece of fine oval gold tinsel. Take several turns about the shank with the oval tinsel to form a gold tag. Tie off and cut the tinsel.

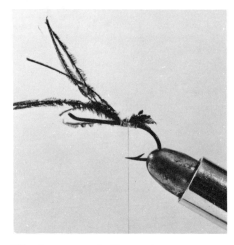

Tie in several fibers from a peacock's body quill. The number of fibers depends on the size of the fly and hook. Clip the excess quill material.

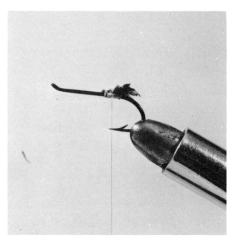

Again tie in the fine oval gold tinsel below the point where the peacock quill fibers are tied in. Next, bring your tying thread forward to almost the middle of the body and tie in the gold floss body material.

Wrap the floss about the shank, forming a smooth tapering cover. Tie off, taking care to leave material for the underwing.

The gold floss underwing should be tied in at the top of the shank without cutting and retying in. Anchor the floss well to keep it from unwrapping.

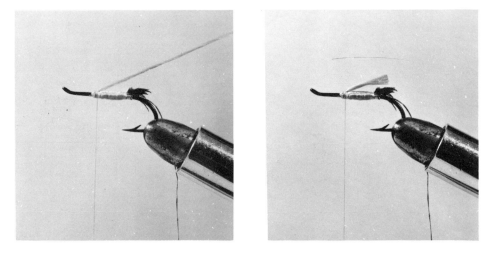

Clip the floss underwing so that it is slightly shorter than the end of the peacock tail. No effort should be made to keep the floss underwing from unraveling.

Take several strands of peacock herl from a tail feather, pinch off the weak fragile tips, and tie in below the secondary wing. Twist the herl into a single strand and wind about the shank, completing the body. Care should be taken to allow for the insertion of wing and hackle without crowding the head.

With the body now complete, spiral the oval gold tinsel up the full length of the body. The tinsel should be wound on in the opposite direction to the floss and herl. This adds strength and further binds the materials together.

Reverse the fly in the vise and select some soft grizzly saddle hackle. Tie in so that the tips almost touch the barb of the hook. Clip fiber butts.

Return the fly to its upright position and place a spot of cement at the point where the hackle is tied in. The cement keeps thread from slipping and materials from becoming loose.

The wing of the Rusty Rat is made from the guard hairs from a gray fox. The object here is to stack the hairs so that they stand wing-like. If hairs are tied on in one bunch, it is exceedingly difficult, if not impossible, to obtain the desired standing effect. To obtain it, tie in the guard hairs in three groups. Place a drop of cement on the butt portion of the hair, just forward of the knot, to anchor it.

Complete the head. All that remains is to apply several coats of lacquer so that the spaces and ridges are completely filled in. Let each coat dry before applying the next.

DARK MYSTRY

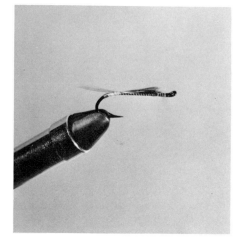

Tie in the oval gold tinsel tag, the fluorescent orange floss sac, and blue dun hen hackle fibers for the tail. Note that the tail fibers extend slightly upward in angle from the hook's shank.

Next, tie in a few strands of black ostrich herl and wind on to form the butt. Then, tie in some tan floss for the body and a strand of oval gold tinsel for the rib. Wrap the floss, taking care to taper the body. With the floss installed, form the rib.

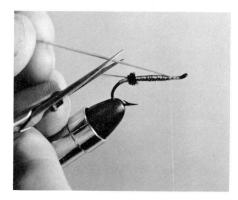

Tie in two matching spotted turkey quills for the wing. Clip the excess butt material.

Tie in several strands of orange and red fluorescent floss to make up the underwing. Clip to desired length.

Tie in legs by taking a few strands of guinea hen hackle and putting them into position. For ease of application, you can reverse the fly in the vise so that the fly is belly up.

Whip finish the head and lacquer. The Dark Mystry is now ready for the stream.

Tying flies to meet low-water conditions can best be done in two ways. In fact, it isn't a bad idea to have some of both with you. The first type of low-water fly is tied small on a regular size hook. The fish is presented with a small-looking lure which has the hooking and holding power of a larger size hook. The second method is tying low-water flies on small hooks. The small hook gives the fly a completely different action in the water than that of the first type using larger and heavier hooks. Low-water flies are usually much sparser in the amount of materials used. They may or may not have all of the materials called for in the standard pattern versions. If all of the materials are used, they are used in much smaller quantities. A slim silhouette is desired of low-water flies.

Up till now, wet flies have been the main topic of discussion. But there is no reason not to take along some dry trout flies. For larger dry patterns, light-wire, salmon, dry-fly hooks can be used. At times, such flies have proved to be quite effective, especially on clear streams, during low-water conditions, when the water is not moving very much. Your dry-fly box should include some spiders, parachutes, and hoppers. Don't be afraid to tie them to the large size hooks.

Another good dry-fly type is the Wulff patterns. They were originally designed for trout but have since proved excellent for salmon. These were the first dry flies to incorporate the use of deer hair and/or bucktail in wings and tails. Deer hair has the property of being hollow. When tied in, air is trapped, which greatly aids in the flotation. They are ideal for fishing the floating fly in fast, rough currents. Deer hair is also quite durable, and flies made with this material will hold up considerably better than regular trout flies made from standard materials.

Another use of deer hair is spinning it about the hook à la bass bug style. This is another Harry Darbee creation which has proved very successful on trout and salmon. I imagine that a few have even been thrown at some bass. It goes by the apt moniker of Rat-Faced McDougall. It is as tough a fly as its name indicates.

RAT-FACED McDOUGALL DRY SALMON FLY

Tail: Fibers from a ginger saddle hackle
Body: Light tan-colored deer hair
Wings: White calf tail
Hackle: Stiff ginger hackle

Begin the dry fly in the usual way by tying in the ginger tail. With the large-size flies, deer hair can be substituted. With the tail securely into position, take a bunch of deer hair about an inch in length (since the light tan color is desired, clip the tip portion of the hair so that the portion near the skin can be utilized) and spin it about the shank. Tie off each bunch of spun hair, and compress it toward the rear.

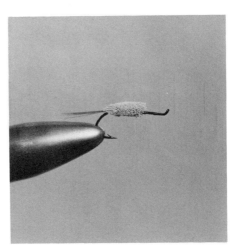

Spin the hair about the shank until half of the hook shank is covered. The body is now ready to be trimmed.

Take a long-bladed scissors and trim the body so that the back of the body is domed and the belly flat.

Select a bunch of hair from a calf's tail and tie in the wings.

With the hair securely tied into position, clip excess material.

Stand the wings upright and separate into two sections. Anchor
them firmly into place. Tie in two
stiff ginger hackles. Wrap the
hackles fore and aft of the wing
so that it fills the space between
wing and body.

The dry salmon fly head is much
smaller than the same wet fly and
the head should not be jammed
close to the eye of the hook. Apply
several coats of lacquer to the head.

Nymph fishing for salmon is an area which is just beginning to be explored. This is an ideal low-water method of taking fish, especially when
they seem to be interested in subsurface food. As parr and grilse, they
depend on such food for a good portion of their diet.

The greatest success to date has been with nymphs which imitate through
pulsations caused by body materials and leg action. And they have proved
to be most successful at low-water levels, and/or when the flow is slow.
Nymphs do not look like regular salmon patterns and may prove better
under specific conditions than do other salmon fly types. One person who is
doing work in the nymph area is Charles De Feo. He has met with much
success, and I have illustrated some of his favorite patterns.

In tying salmon flies, there is a great tendency for the dresser to use more
materials than are necessary. As with other types of flies, when this is done,
it kills the action of the fly. Fur and feather fibers should be able to pulsate

when worked. Our goal is to give as much life to our lures as possible, not to see how much material we can put on the hook. Subsurface water currents help the fly's action. When a fly, wet or dry, is overdressed, there is a tendency for the fibers to collect and retain water—much the same as a paint brush. With sparsely tied flies, there are fewer fibers for the water molecules to attach to, and the fibers have more freedom of movement.

HAT PINS

Hat pins can be made of salmon flies. The pins are available from Veniard's in England in gold or silver finish. The flies are tied in the usual manner but because of the large size more materials are used than with regular flies.

Some say that salmon fishing is on the way out. I agree that the salmon returning to their rivers to spawn are down in number. This is because the fishing fleets of several nations have found out where the fish are during their schooling grounds, and have done a complete job of catching them. It is up to us as anglers and sportsmen to bring as much pressure to bear as possible so that those who are in control of these fleets can be forced to stop their rape of the sea before it is too late. The Atlantic salmon is far too noble a game fish to be obliterated. Should this happen, tying salmon flies would become nothing more than an art form.

▲▲▲▲▲ CHAPTER 8 ▲▲▲▲▲

UPSTREAM AND DOWN

This chapter is intended for those who are interested in improving their angling methods and techniques. It does not contain information on how to cast, tie leaders,or other such basics. I have left that to my angling brethren, who have included such information in their earlier works. What will be included are tips which I have worked out over the years or which have been passed on to me by others. All have made my day on the stream more enjoyable and successful. With this in mind, why not stand at my side while I fish a few pools.

Let's go fishing!

All streams contain signs and guideposts for the experienced fisherman. These reveal where the fish are lying, what food they are taking, and which of the many fishing techniques they will respond to. The better one understands the outdoors, the more fruitfully will he be rewarded for his angling efforts.

We live some distance from the area where we will be angling (about 75 miles), and have not heard what local water conditions are to be like.

Because of this, we will be taking our waders instead of our hip boots. It goes without saying that both waders and hipboots should be felt-bottomed. You are inviting disaster with the plain rubber, cleated ones. I also prefer stocking-foot waders and wading shoes to the one-piece unit. I realize that they may be a bit more of a bother. However, in terms of sure-footedness they make the difference and are worth the inconvenience.

We have arrived at our fishing spot, and are in the process of rigging up. The best way of running the line through the guides is by doubling the leader and line at the point of the knot and pushing them both through together—not by trying to thread the guides with the leader's tippet.

We are rigged up, and standing quietly at streamside surveying a likely piece of water. It is early in the season, and as of yet no fish are rising: The water temperature is much too cold. Past experience has shown us that trout will take minnows and nymphs under these conditions.

Our stream is clear but fast. The water is a bit high. And it is just beginning to recede from a steady, all-day spring rain two days ago. At this particular spot, it is a wide, boulder-strewn run containing good pocket water. At its deepest, it is six to eight feet deep; ideal for holding large and, we hope, hungry trout.

Our first choice is a Thunder Creek Silver Shiner tied on a number six hook. This is attached to our eight-foot leader to which we have tied a two-and-a-half-foot 4X tippet. From bank to bank, the stream is about twenty-five feet wide. Ankle deep in water, we wet the fly without causing a disturbance, then make a roll cast across and slightly upstream. The cast is short, so we apply no action to the fly, allowing the currents to carry it as they will. After the cast, we strip a few more feet of line through the guides. This too is taken by the currents. We pay no attention to drag. At the end, when there is no more line, the currents straighten out our line, leader, and fly so that it is directly below us downstream. At this point it is a good idea to let the fly rest in the currents—the longer the better. Usually impatience dictates how long the fly is allowed to rest. It is twitched a few times, retrieved, and another cast made. Gradually casts are lengthened (or shortened) to be worked over likely looking spots as we move slowly downstream.

We lose the first but take the second fish. With the first we were a bit too fast in setting the hook and pulled the fly away from the fish. If the hook is sharp, all that's needed to set the hook is a simple raising of the rod tip. For sharpening hooks, I always carry one of my wife's emery nail boards.

We clean the fish caught at streamside as soon as we have finished fishing the run in order to prevent spoilage. This is done by taking a small penknife and inserting the point in the anal pore. The knife is then moved forward to the gills. If the point is inserted just deep enough to cut through the belly and no deeper, none of the organs will be punctured. They can then be removed in mass. Also remove the gills, but leave the head. If sweet grass or ferns are available, line your creel with it and wet it down to keep your fish from drying out.

A side benefit which comes from cleaning your fish is being able to perform an autopsy to determine what he has been feeding on. This can easily be done by carefully slitting his stomach open. The flies and/or minnows most rcently taken will have less of an opportunity to be broken down by the stomach acids. These are the contents to work with. The fish which we caught has some large brownish-gray nymphs which are partially digested.

Since the water temperature has risen from the sun's heat, the next fly we tie on is a nymph. But before getting back to fishing, we decide to boil some water for tea.

We agreed earlier with our partner to meet and compare notes. In so doing, both help each other and the end result is more fish and fun. We are actually a team, working independently of one another. Very often, one of us will have found the right angling combination which the other had over-looked for some reason.

Information is exchanged. Our partner took three fish, keeping the largest of the three. It is a sixteen-inch brown trout, a deep heavy fish in full-dress colors. His conclusions correspond with ours: Nymphs should produce, now that the water temperature has risen. The tea cuts the icy chill in our bodies; the last is drunk and we head back to the river.

This time, we head upstream, to some slower-moving water. Nature has made some natural step-like pools in the side of a high, gradually sloping mountain. At the first pool we come to, the water is coming over a step and drops about three feet into a long glide. At the tail end of the pool, rocks break up the water into riffles. An ideal situation for fishing a Krom March Brown Nymph.

Our first casts are made from a position in which the fly can cover water across and downstream for us. At the end of the first cast, just above where the riffles begin, we see a flashing fish. No take. We cast again, this time a bit more upstream. We are deepening our drift and at the same time fishing soem new water. This time at the end of the cast there is a tugging-type strike from a moving fish.

The rod tip is raised and drag is applied with our fingers. Our purpose here is to keep the fish out of the riffles just below. After setting the hook by raising the rod tip, we lower it so that it makes an angle of 30 to 45 degrees with the surface of the water. This is the rod position from which we will play the fish. A high rod while playing a fish very often leads to a broken tip. By giving as little line as possible and at the same time applying rod pressure we keep the fish from heading downstream. He makes a flashing run upstream. The rod tip is dropped; and we give him line for his run. He is above us, where he not only has us to contend with but the current as well. A few more brief runs and the fish is brought to net.

It is a brookie, lightly hooked, and so we return it. First, we wet our hands to keep the slime from sticking. The trout is held gently at its mid-section, the hook removed, and the fish faced upstream. Usually the fish will dart away as soon as it is released. If the fish seems a bit sluggish after the ordeal, gently move it back and forth in the water. This puts the sparkle back in the trout. It should then move off under its own steam.

The same procedure is followed on the other pools with the results of at least one fish per pool hooked and landed. By lunch time, there are four good fish in the creel with a total of nine hooked and landed. We just have time for lunch before the flies begin coming off the water.

A hot lunch has a rejuvenating effect. Whenever possible, we carry a tank-type burner stove. They provide enough heat to cook soup or boil water for tea and instant coffee rapidly. They are light in weight, easy to pack, and don't take up a great deal of room. There is nothing like a hot lunch after standing in water just above the freezing level all morning. Pack along a couple of sandwiches, fruit, and some cookies or candy. It helps to make the trip a success.

During the later months, when it becomes too hot to fish during midday, we usually break with a nap after lunch. However, today, because it is early in the season, the flies should be coming off the water in the early afternoon. That is, if there is going to be any hatch at all. Because of the likelihood of the hatch occurring early in the day, not at dusk, we fish through and knock off when the sun begins to cool the water.

Before the rain a few days ago, a local friend passed the word that there had been a small hatch between 1:00 and 3:00 P.M. every afternoon in the previous week. This was what we were waiting for; the time was right for us to get back to the river.

Along with the exchange of information at lunch, we discussed the water we fished in the morning. When we returned to the river, we were heading downstream. I wanted to try some dry-fly fishing which I term Trac III Trout Fishing; my companion wanted to try some nymphs, until conditions dictated change.

Trac III Trout Fishing combines several new combinations of angling techniques and fly tying. At its best, Trac III is the wedded combination of a sparsely tied, non-absorbing dry fly and fishing the dry fly downstream. In the two seasons which this new technique has been tested it has proved extremely successful. It is also ideal for large and small stream alike, though especially for small streams which are overhung with foliage to the point of making casting a near impossibility.

The Trac III dry fly is our dry fly tied with a minimum of materials and hackle. The materials chosen should be as waterproof as possible. Wings and tails should be made with deer or similar hair which trap air and help float the fly. For the body, the fur used usually comes from water animals or animals which have a lot of natural oils in their skin. Hackle should be stiff and non-absorbing.

The Trac III technique imitates the natural rise of an insect to surface. It is fished across and downstream. If conditions are such that anything but an ultra-short cast will find you hung up in a tree, make the cast short and then strip line from the reel, allowing it to flow through the guides. Strip just enough line to reach your objective downstream.

Trac I is the downstream cast. The fly is pretty much free of drag until most of the line is extended. Trac I is an ideal way of reaching fish that are impossible to cast to when fishing the dry fly upstream. Usually, in regular dry-fly fishing when the float is extended to where drag begins, the fly is picked up from the water and another cast is made. In Trac III dry-fly fishing, we leave the fly on the water. Trac II begins when the line is extended and drag sets in to the fly and line. Usually, the fly is pulled across stream in the path of an arc. If a trout has been suspicious of a fraud during Trac I, when the fly begins to move away from him during Trac II it is often enough to make him strike. I have had fish literally race each other and fight over the fly. The winner is usually the loser.

At the end of Trac II, the arc-like movement brings the fly and line directly below you, when facing downstream. Most always, the currents pull the fly beneath the surface, regardless of what materials are used in the lure's construction. This begins Trac III.

Trac III begins with the fly submerged downstream from the angler. The natural urge is for the angler to pull his fly from beneath the water, false cast, and make another cast. With my method, we let the fly stay submerged. The longer the rest underwater, the better one's chance of success if a fish is suspicious or on the verge of being spooked. After a reasonable resting period, the fly is twitched ever so lightly, Manipulating the line without using the rod tip will produce the right action. The fly is again rested. Repeat the procedure again. If there is no strike by this time, use the hand retrieve in bringing the fly in.

The Trac II method of trout fishing manipulates the fly so that it imitates a floating fly during Trac I. As it arcs during Trac II, it imitates a fly about to become airborne. Trac III imitates an insect's lifelike motions to get to the surface. The slight twitching produces a bobbing effect underwater.

The materials which go into the fly are extremely important as they must take a great deal of abuse being underwater so much of the cast. Specific patterns do not seem to be so important, as long as the fly is of the imitative, rather than the attractive, variety.

Several times during the testing period, I had the opportunity to use Trac III during a hatch. I had equal success with a fly imitating a hatch and one in which there was no resemblance. This played little, if any, part in getting a fish to strike. What seemed to be the controlling factor was the fly's action, in or on the water. However, to utilize this technique to its maximum advantage it must be correlated with the lure. As stated, fly construction and materials play as much a part as line control. All help in giving the fly the appearance of action and realism.

For the angler who is new to the sport, I would like to suggest that he stick to the smaller streams and rivers. He will catch more fish than on a large river and learn more of the world in which the trout lives. Big water has a way of clouding an angling situation so that it appears as if luck was in full control. Good fishing!